Dear Sarah,

I know you enjoy making cocktails. I would love to try one of these sometime!

Love,
Nathan

zero-proof cocktails

zero-proof cocktails

alcohol-free beverages for every occasion

LIZ SCOTT

photography by Sheri Giblin

TEN SPEED PRESS
Berkeley | Toronto

ACKNOWLEDGMENTS

THANK YOU TO EVERYONE at Ten Speed Press for your tremendous support and enthusiasm. In particular, I must pay tribute to my terrific editor, Genoveva Llosa for her encouragement, patience, and vision. Thanks also to my agent, Coleen O'Shea, my publicist, Susan Burnash, and Larry Chilnick for their continual support. My dear friends (and eager taste testers) Jimmy, Jennifer, and Anna, I couldn't have done it without you. And of course, Baby, my feline companion who knows that every hour is "happy hour" as long as a peacock feather is involved.

Ten Speed Press
PO Box 7123
Berkeley, California 94707
www.tenspeed.com

Distributed in Australia by Simon and Schuster Australia, in Canada by Ten Speed Press Canada, in New Zealand by Southern Publishers Group, in South Africa by Real Books, and in the United Kingdom and Europe by Publishers Group UK.

Cover and text design by Toni Tajima
Food styling by Dan Becker
Prop styling by Christine Wolheim
Photography assistance by Stacy Ventura
Digital assistance by Sherry Heck

Library of Congress Cataloging-in-Publication Data

Scott, Liz, 1957-
  Zero-proof cocktails : alcohol-free beverages for every occasion / Liz Scott ; photography by Sheri Giblin.
       p. cm.
  Includes index.
  Summary: "A collection of 100 recipes for nonalcoholic aperitifs, mocktails, martinis, infusions, and wine alternatives"—Provided by publisher.
  ISBN 978-1-58008-959-3
  1. Non-alcoholic cocktails. I. Title.
  TX815.S43 2009
  641.8'75—dc22

                              2008038711

Printed in China
First printing, 2009

1 2 3 4 5 6 7 8 9 10 — 13 12 11 10 09

CONTENTS

INTRODUCTION

WHEN ENTERTAINING, every host aspires to create an atmosphere of conviviality and cheer punctuated with delicious food and drink, and at today's parties and gatherings, cocktails are more popular than ever. Originally, *cocktail* described an alcoholic beverage consisting of spirits with splashes of soda or water and medicinal bitters, but eventually it came to be known as any type of mixed alcoholic drink. Today, the definition of *cocktail* is far more inclusive. From aperitifs to nightcaps, just about any specialty drink can fall under this umbrella.

Whether at a casual get-together or a formal event, providing guests with a selection of innovative cocktails is surely the sign of a thoughtful and creative host. But catering to every guest's likes and needs can at times be a daunting task. One of the challenges today's host may face is the expectation that alcohol-free beverages will go beyond a simple club soda. Guests who need or prefer to avoid alcohol, either temporarily or permanently, and who request something "soft" or "buzz-free," may anticipate a more interesting alternative. In the past, that request was met with a ginger ale or, at best, a Shirley Temple. But these days, bar chefs—creative bartenders who make use of delectable ingredients from the kitchen—are producing inspired mocktails and virgin renditions of famous drinks, and fine dining establishments have even begun to include alcohol-free beverage pairings on their menus. This new and exciting trend has opened up the possibilities for nondrinkers and their hosts, raising the bar for creativity and innovation.

As a chef, caterer, and nondrinker myself, I'm thrilled that this new approach has taken hold. Abstinent guests are less likely to feel frustrated by a lack of beverage choices or left out while others sip from fancy cocktail glasses and marvel at pretty garnishes. Unfortunately, most of the alcohol-free drink books currently available are less than inspired, with a focus on overly sweet mocktails that are nothing more than a mixer without the alcohol. In order to create truly enticing zero-proof drinks that people will enjoy, we must think "outside the bottle" and incorporate exciting ingredients and flavor combinations that will overshadow the absence of alcohol. This has been my approach to cooking without alcohol as well, and it's the driving force behind every recipe here, from the remarkably satisfying Black Cherry Kina aperitif to the quintessential Caruso Comeback nightcap. Every cocktail has an interesting and unexpected twist that will surprise and delight your guests with each sip. And best of all, all of the recipes are easy to prepare and provide everything you need to know about ingredients, servings, and presentation. From now on, when you or your guests are abstaining, festivity and fun won't be off the menu.

INGREDIENTS AND EQUIPMENT

MANY OF THE COMMON INGREDIENTS and pieces of equipment in a traditional bar are also useful when preparing zero-proof cocktails. Some of these, as well as a few less-well-known items, bear mentioning to help you prepare your bar and kitchen for making the drink recipes in this book. The Resources section in the back provides websites for further information on some of the more unusual ingredients.

Bitters
Cocktails often contain a dash of bitters, astringent-tasting drink enhancements usually made from herbs and fruit. Not all bitters are alcohol free, however, so if imbibers must completely shun alcohol, bitters such as Angostura should not be used. Fee Brothers' high-quality line of bitters, which includes grapefruit and orange bitters, also contains a small amount of alcohol, but you can use them if total abstention from alcohol isn't necessary. Stirrings' blood orange bitters, recommended for many of the recipes in this book, is completely free of alcohol and widely available.

Blender
An electric blender is necessary for a smooth and creamy consistency in certain drinks, and is particularly useful for drinks made with pureed fruit. If you'll be serving both alcohol-free and traditional blended cocktails at the same event, it's a good idea to use two separate blenders, as some nondrinkers may be sensitive to the residual taste of alcohol in the pitcher.

Citrus Twists and Slices

Use a channel knife or citrus peeler to make 1/4-inch-wide strips of citrus peel, such as lemon, lime, and orange. The oil of the zest contributes a wonderful intense flavor to drinks and the strips make a pretty garnish. Lemon and lime slices are common cocktail garnishes and are handy to combine with other fruit pieces or ingredients on cocktail picks and decorative skewers.

Cocktail Shaker

Most martinis and mixed drinks are shaken or stirred in a cocktail shaker, which results in excellent chilling as well as thorough blending. The strainer holds the ice back as the drink is poured so the cocktail doesn't become diluted. Most shakers come with their own strainer and top. If you're entertaining a large number of guests and offering several different cocktails, you may want to have two or three on hand.

Dealcoholized Wine and Beer

It's important to note that so-called alcohol-free versions of wine and beer can still contain 0.5 percent alcohol by law. For those who cannot imbibe its best to steer clear of these products. If, however, a small amount of alcohol is not an issue for guests, you can substitute these for alcohol-free sparkling grape juices, for instance, and other similar beverages.

Extracts and Essences

Typical baking extracts, such as vanilla, contain at least 35 percent alcohol by volume, and certain flavors may contain even more. When extracts are called for in the recipes that follow, alcohol-free versions, which use glycerin as a base, are specified. You can find them at Trader Joe's or natural food stores, or order them online. If small amounts of alcohol don't present a problem, you can use regular extracts. Essences, such as rose water or orange blossom water, don't contain alcohol.

Food Processor

Valuable for breaking down fruits and vegetables that will be strained, this modern kitchen essential will alleviate tedious chopping. However, it won't yield a creamy consistency for beverages, as a blender will.

Fruit Juices

Although freshly squeezed juices are a delicious luxury to offer guests when entertaining, convenience may sometimes win out. Unless a recipe specifically calls for freshly squeezed, feel free to take advantage of the many refrigerated, canned, bottled, and frozen products available. Rose's Lime Juice is a unique product; it's heavily sweetened and more like a syrup than a fruit juice. It's available in supermarkets in the beverage aisle and should be used when called for, as there's no good substitute for it.

Garnishes

From olives to lemon slices to chocolate shavings, a cocktail garnish can add an immediate touch of sophistication or fun. Simple garnishes are included in most of the drink recipes, but feel free to create your own when the inspiration hits. Stainless steel cocktail picks and skewers add a further hint of luxury over disposable wooden or plastic varieties.

Glassware

Many cocktails are associated with a specific shape of glass, such as a highball glass or a champagne flute. The recipes indicate which glass to use, but if you aren't stocked with myriad barware, don't worry. Any type of attractive glass can be substituted. When serving zero-proof cocktails to guests who are strictly sober, it's prudent to inquire if a cocktail presentation might be uncomfortable for them, in which case you can use a less-suggestive glass.

Grenadine

Long before the current popularity of pomegranates, grenadine—which is a pomegranate-flavored syrup—was added to cocktails for its vibrant color and flavor. Nearly all varieties of grenadine available today are alcohol free, but some may contain a small amount of alcohol. Surprisingly, some are even pomegranate free! So read the label carefully to make sure you are getting the real thing. When pomegranate syrup is called for in a recipe, use an ethnic variety or commercial brand such as Monin's rather than pouring from the grenadine bottle. The difference is subtle but important to the taste of the drink.

Herbs

Fresh herbs add distinctive flavors and aromas to infusions and syrups. Dried herbs simply don't provide the same fragrance and taste, so don't substitute unless you absolutely must. Fresh herb sprigs make attractive garnishes, particularly in cocktails that contain their essence.

Ice

Regular ice cubes are fine to use for shaking or stirring cocktails when the cubes will be strained out. Crushed ice works better in a blender. In nonblended drinks that call for crushed ice, it's important for presentation. Use a manual or electric ice crusher, or place ice cubes in a plastic bag and crush them with a mallet or rolling pin.

Muddler

Made of wood so as not to scratch glass, this handy tool is necessary for mojitos and other drinks that require mashing ingredients together to release their juices and essential oils. In a pinch, a ceramic mortar and pestle can be used.

Seltzer

Flavored seltzers add a nice hint of flavor and fizz when used as a final splash in many types of cocktails. When plain seltzer is called for, club soda or sparkling water can be substituted.

Sodas

Sodas made from natural ingredients have a definite place in zero-proof drink making, particularly the not-too-sweet Italian varieties. It's valuable to have a variety on hand for pouring or mixing when you're entertaining or serving guests with different preferences. When sodas are called for in the recipes, it's fine to substitute diet or decaffeinated versions.

Sugar

When sugar is called for in the recipes, particularly for making syrups, white granulated sugar is the type to choose. For mixing cold drinks, choose superfine sugar, as it dissolves quickly. Other types of sugar, such as brown sugar, raw sugar, or vanilla sugar are specified for certain recipes because their unique flavor or appearance complements that beverage.

Syrups

Flavored sugar syrups are excellent for mimicking the color and taste of many liqueurs. Monin and Torani are the main producers of these types of products, which are often used in cafés for flavoring coffee and tea, but you may run across other brands, and all are fine to use. Some of the recipes call for making your own syrup because the ultimate flavor is unique or complex and not readily available in a premade syrup. If, however, you can find a comparable commercial syrup and wish to use it to cut back on preparation time, feel free to substitute.

Tea

The mouth-puckering tannins in tea make it an excellent ingredient for mocktails and copycat wines. You can use regular tea or decaffeinated, and loose leaf or tea bags, depending on what you have on hand. Herbal teas, which are usually naturally free of caffeine, are especially ideal for achieving unique or exotic flavors.

Whipped Cream

Some cocktails call for a whipped cream garnish. To make whipped cream, beat chilled heavy cream with an electric mixer until soft or stiff peaks form. If you prefer sweetened whipped cream, add 1 to 3 tablespoons of confectioners' sugar per cup of cream while beating. Prepare up to 1 hour before serving and keep refrigerated.

chapter 1

elixirs and aperitifs

The traditional glass of sherry or vermouth, long popular as a before-dinner drink, has given way to an array of creative concoctions and rediscovered liqueurs and tonics. For the versatile host, making zero-proof versions of these types of cocktails has never been easier or more exciting. From unusual fruit juices and syrups to alcohol-free bitters and infusions, countless extraordinary ingredients can be combined to create an assortment of delicious alcohol-free elixirs and aperitifs that will please every palate and begin any get-together with sophistication and novelty.

Aperitifs, as well as elixirs, or remedy drinks, were originally designed as medicinal beverages, most often made by infusing spirits with herbs and spices and served to stimulate the appetite. Today they're enjoying a comeback in entertaining, as they provide the perfect prelude to an afternoon or evening of fine food by priming the palate and creating an atmosphere of warmth and hospitality. Literally translated from the Latin *aperire*, meaning "to open," an aperitif will start off your entertaining with real style, no matter what the occasion.

old-fashioned barley water

Popular since the nineteenth century as a restorative for people with a weak constitution, this elixir has also long been used as a thirst quencher for athletes and is still served at the annual tennis tournament in Wimbledon, England. Keep some barley water on hand for gulping after strenuous runs and workouts, or for under-the-weather guests or family members who crave something refreshing without the buzz or fizz.

SERVES 2

¹/₂ cup pearl barley

4 cups spring water

3 tablespoons superfine sugar, or more to taste

Juice of 1 lemon

2 lemon slices, for garnish

Rinse the barley in a sieve under cold running water for about 1 minute, until the water runs clear. Combine the spring water and sugar in a saucepan and bring to a boil, stirring occasionally. Stir in the barley and return to a boil. Lower the heat, cover, and simmer for 20 minutes.

Strain the barley water into a pitcher or jug and let cool to room temperature. Stir in the lemon juice, taste, and add more sugar if you like. Chill before serving in tumblers, with or without ice, garnished with the lemon slices.

herbal cleanse infusion

Instead of sipping from uninspired bottles of plain water, keep this terrific cleansing spa water on hand to flush toxins away with the healing virtues of cucumber, lemon, and herbs. Perfect for anyone who wants to look and feel radiant and refreshed. Serve this infusion well chilled and without ice.

SERVES 2

1 (1-liter) bottle purified water

6 thin slices unpeeled cucumber

$^1/_2$ lemon, thinly sliced and seeded

2 (2-inch) sprigs of mint

1 sprig of basil

Splash of grenadine

2 lemon slices, for garnish

Pour the water into a large pitcher and add the cucumber, lemon, and herbs. Chill for at least 2 hours. Strain, then pour into 2 large tumblers, add a splash of grenadine, and serve garnished with the lemon slices.

pimm and proper

When mad dogs and Englishmen go out in the noonday sun, there's always a glass of ice-cold Pimm's Cup on offer to quench a ferocious thirst. A British classic since 1823, Pimm's No. 1, a gin-based aperitif infused with herbs and fruit, was originally created as a health drink. Its unique flavor mixes well with lemonade, ginger ale, or sparkling water. Here, an infusion of herbs and a dash of nonalcoholic blood orange bitters help recreate this classic. Use the extra syrup to make a thirst quencher anytime you need one.

SERVES 1

Ice

3 tablespoons Herbal Infusion (see recipe below)

1 cup sparkling water or club soda, well chilled

Dash of blood orange bitters

1 lemon slice, for garnish

1 cucumber spear, for garnish

Fill a tall glass with ice. Add the Herbal Infusion, sparkling water, and bitters. Stir, insert the lemon slice and cucumber spear, and serve.

herbal infusion

1 chamomile tea bag

$^{1}/_{4}$ cup fresh herbs such as spearmint, lemon thyme, and pineapple sage

$^{1}/_{2}$ cup boiling water

$^{1}/_{2}$ cup sugar

Combine the tea bag and herbs in a small bowl. Pour in the boiling water and steep for 15 minutes. Strain into a small saucepan, add the sugar, and bring to a boil, stirring until the sugar dissolves. Lower the heat and simmer for 5 minutes, until slightly thickened. Cool before using. Makes about $^{1}/_{2}$ cup. Refrigerated, it will keep for up to 2 weeks.

cucumber cup

The fresh, clean taste of cucumber is featured in this perfect aperitif for summer entertaining. A little lime and a bit of sugar bring out the full flavor of this ubiquitous garden vegetable. Use regular waxy cucumbers for making the juice, but garnish with slices of seedless English cucumber, a tastier and prettier cousin. Those who drink alcohol and are gimlet fans can add a shot of gin or vodka.

SERVES 4

2 large waxy cucumbers, peeled, cut into chunks, and chilled

1 tablespoon freshly squeezed lime juice

1^1/$_2$ tablespoons superfine sugar

Pinch of salt

1 cup crushed ice

4 lime slices, for garnish

4 English cucumber slices, for garnish

Put the cucumber chunks in a food processor fitted with the steel blade and puree until smooth. Pour the puree through a fine-mesh sieve into a bowl, pressing on the solids to extract all of the juice. Discard the solids.

Whisk in the lime juice, sugar, and salt. Transfer to a blender, add the ice, and puree briefly until slushy. Immediately pour into 4 cocktail glasses and serve garnished with the lime and cucumber slices.

tomato essence infusion

Ripe, juicy tomatoes are the key to this intensely flavored aperitif that can be sipped and savored on its own or accompanied by salty nuts or olives. Extremely soft tomatoes that have passed their prime for salads are ideal here. Heirloom tomatoes or the unfortunately named Ugly tomatoes are particularly good choices because of their full flavor. Feel free to add a splash of vodka for anyone who drinks alcohol.

SERVES 4

8 large, soft, vine-ripened tomatoes, cored

1 teaspoon sea salt

Dash of freshly ground white pepper

1 teaspoon superfine sugar

Juice of ¹/₂ lemon

2 large basil leaves

4 small grape tomatoes, halved, for garnish

4 sprigs of basil, for garnish

Coarsely chop the tomatoes then put them, along with their juices, in a food processor fitted with the steel blade. Add the salt, pepper, sugar, and lemon juice and process until well chopped and smooth, about 30 seconds. Place a fine-mesh sieve over a large bowl and line the sieve with a double layer of cheesecloth. Pour the tomato mixture into the sieve, then gather together the ends of the cheesecloth and secure them with string. Place in the refrigerator and allow the liquid to drain for at least 4 hours.

Lightly press the cheesecloth to extract all of the flavorful liquid. Discard the solids. Crush the basil slightly with your fingers, add to the bowl, and chill for at least 1 hour longer.

To serve, remove the basil leaves, then pour the tomato essence through a fine-mesh sieve (to remove any last bits of pulp) into a small pitcher or decanter. Pour into 4 double shot or vodka glasses, and serve garnished with the grape tomatoes and basil sprigs on a cocktail pick.

health nut's aperitif

If your nondrinking guests happen to be passionately health conscious, they'll love this delicious aperitif, which is perfect for any casual dinner gathering. Packed with vitamin C and enhanced with the bite of fresh ginger, this concoction is both nourishing and delicious. No need to juice the carrots yourself; just seek out a high-quality, fresh carrot juice in the refrigerated section of your supermarket and away you go. Serve with a platter of vegetable crudités and drink to your health.

SERVES 1

1 thin slice fresh gingerroot

1 (1-inch) piece fennel

1 tablespoon freshly squeezed lemon juice

$1/2$ cup fresh carrot juice

$1/2$ cup orange juice

$1/2$ cup pineapple juice

Ice

Fennel frond, for garnish

Put the gingerroot, fennel, and lemon juice in a cocktail shaker and muddle until crushed and fragrant. Add the remaining juices and ice and shake until combined and well chilled. Strain into an old-fashioned glass and serve garnished with the fennel frond.

blueberry cobbler

Traditional cobbler cocktails make use of seasonal fruit as a topping over a tumbler of crushed ice and liquor. Here, delicious blueberry juice provides the base, and a lemon-lime seltzer assists in toning down its sweetness. If you can't find straight blueberry juice, substitute one of the popular combination juices, such as pomegranate blueberry. Serve this cobbler on its own or with appetizer nibbles such as sugar-glazed nuts, and provide a straw for slurping and a spoon for capturing the succulent blueberries.

SERVES 1

$^1/_2$ **cup blueberry juice**

Crushed ice

Splash of lemon-lime seltzer

$^1/_4$ **cup blueberries, washed and stemmed**

Pour the blueberry juice into a tumbler and add crushed ice almost to the top of the glass. Add a good splash of lemon-lime seltzer and top with the blueberries. Insert a long straw and iced tea spoon before serving.

a-pear-itif

This delightfully refreshing predinner drink, with its bouquet of fresh, ripe pears, will be popular among nondrinkers and drinkers alike. Softly scented pear-infused white balsamic vinegar, which can be found at specialty food stores and well-stocked grocery stores, will add that certain something to the sweet mix of nectar and sparkling juice. Kristian Regale's sparkling pear juice is the perfect choice here and is also often available in supermarkets and at specialty grocers. If it's difficult to find, another brand, such as Izze, could be substituted. Pear-friendly accompaniments such as crumbled blue cheese and glazed walnuts create the perfect pairing. For the pear garnish, Bosc and Anjou are good choices; be sure to slice it just before serving, so it doesn't brown.

SERVES 4

1¹/₃ cups pear nectar, well chilled

1 (750 ml) bottle sparkling pear juice, well chilled

1 tablespoon pear-infused white balsamic vinegar

12 thin pear slices, for garnish

Combine the nectar, juice, and vinegar in a small pitcher and stir well. Divide among 4 wineglasses, and serve each garnished with 3 pear slices on a cocktail pick.

fizzy mint lemonade

This not-too-sweet, lemony aperitif with a hint of mint is a terrific refreshment any time of day, but it's particularly good as a start to an al fresco meal when temperatures are high. A cross between old-fashioned lemonade and the clear and bubbly French-style limonade, this drink is a great alternative to a white wine spritzer. You can make the Lemon Syrup a few days ahead and keep it chilled in the refrigerator. The mint-flecked ice cubes, which can also be prepared days ahead, are also nice to have on hand to provide a special touch when serving sparkling water or spring water to guests.

SERVES 6

Mint Ice

Mint leaves

Spring water

Lemon Syrup

1¹/₂ cups sugar

1¹/₂ cups water

Zest of 2 lemons

Juice of 2 lemons

1 (1-liter) bottle plain seltzer, well chilled

To make the Mint Ice, place a mint leaf in each compartment of an ice cube tray and fill with spring water. Freeze until solid.

To make the Lemon Syrup, combine the sugar, water, and lemon zest in a saucepan and bring to a boil, stirring often. Lower the heat and simmer for 5 minutes, until somewhat thickened. Cool the syrup to room temperature, then stir in the lemon juice, and strain into an airtight container. Chill before using.

To serve, place 2 mint ice cubes in each of 6 large wineglasses, divide the syrup evenly among them, and stir about ³/₄ cup seltzer into each.

black cherry kina

Wine-based aperitifs flavored with quinine are known as quinquinas in France, a name derived from the kina-kina (or cinchona) tree, whose bark provides the distinctive flavor present in quinine, or tonic water. Here, an aromatic Black Cherry Infusion, similar in taste and appearance to a fruity spiced wine, provides the base for a splash of tonic, yielding a predinner drink that can compete with its alcohol-containing quinquina counterparts, such as Dubonnet or Lillet Rouge. Look for black cherry juice with no added sugar in your supermarket or natural food store, where you may also be able to find a black cherry juice concentrate that's reconstituted with water. Since the vanilla bean doesn't need to be opened and scraped, after infusing the juice, rinse and save it for another occasion. Cardamom pods can sometimes be found in the spice section of your supermarket or in many ethnic markets.

SERVES 8

Black Cherry Infusion

2 cups no-sugar-added black cherry juice

$1/2$ vanilla bean

1 (1-inch) piece of orange zest

3 cardamom pods, slightly crushed

Ice

Tonic water

8 orange twists, for garnish

To make the Black Cherry Infusion, heat the black cherry juice in a saucepan over medium-high heat until almost boiling, but don't allow it to boil. Add the vanilla bean, zest, and cardamom, remove from the heat, and infuse for 30 minutes. Strain into a small pitcher or decanter and refrigerate until well chilled.

Divide the infusion among 8 old-fashioned glasses filled with ice. Add a splash of tonic water to each and serve garnished with the orange twists.

bitter orange vesper

Reminiscent of Lillet Blanc, a French fortified wine served as an aperitif, this drink will no doubt intrigue James Bond fans. In the classic film Casino Royale, *007 orders a Vesper martini, in which the traditional vermouth is replaced with Lillet. Slightly sweet, with a tropical aroma and a bitter finish, this Vesper is ideal for sipping before dinner. Its fresh, cleansing effect on the palate will prime guests for the meal to come, while its novelty is likely to stimulate some interesting conversation. This refreshing before-dinner treat is so simple to prepare, there's no reason you can't make one for yourself anytime you like.*

SERVES 1

Ice

1 teaspoon blood orange bitters

1 sprig of mint

¼ cup no-sugar-added white grape juice

Splash of club soda

Orange slice, for garnish

Fill an old-fashioned glass with ice and moisten it with the bitters. Crush the mint between your fingers, then add it to the glass. Pour in the grape juice, add the club soda, and serve garnished with the orange slice.

la strega cocktail

Italy's beloved Strega liqueur, an herbal infusion with a vibrant yellow color from saffron, was typically served after dinner rather than as an aperitif. But with the recent popularity of herbal concoctions as preludes to dinner in the United States, it has found itself happily placed at either end of the meal. The word strega, meaning "witch," harks back to a Lombard legend that claimed witches all over the world would congregate in Benevento, the Italian city where Strega was created. Strega fans agree that the infusion includes hints of fennel and mint, but the rest of the ingredients are a guarded secret. For this nonalcoholic version, a Strega-like syrup made from a collection of aromatic herbs provides the base, while a splash of bitter lemon soda finishes it off in true aperitif fashion.

SERVES 4

Strega Syrup

1 cup water

1 cup sugar

1 bay leaf

2 whole cloves

1/4 teaspoon fennel seeds

1 sprig of mint

2 basil leaves

1 (1-inch) sprig of rosemary

Pinch of saffron threads

Ice

Splash of bitter lemon soda

To make the Strega Syrup, combine the water and sugar in a small saucepan and bring to a boil, stirring often. Add the bay leaf, cloves, fennel seeds, mint, basil, rosemary, and saffron, lower the heat, and simmer for 3 minutes. Cool the syrup to room temperature, then strain it through a fine-mesh sieve into an airtight container and chill before using.

Divide the syrup among 4 old-fashioned glasses. Fill each glass with ice, add a splash of bitter lemon soda, and stir gently before serving.

kira rosso

Inspired by the French aperitif named for the mayor of Dijon, the classic Kir and its many variations have always been a popular start to an evening of fine dining. Traditionally made with crème de cassis, a black currant liqueur, and either white wine or champagne, this version gets its rosy hue from raspberry syrup mingling with a sparkling white grape juice and a garnish of fresh raspberries. Perfectly delicious on its own, this elegant quaff would go equally well with a tray of select hot hors d'ouevres such as cheese puffs or shrimp puffs.

SERVES 6

¹/₃ cup raspberry syrup

1 cup raspberries

1 (750 ml) bottle no-sugar-added sparkling white grape juice, well chilled

Divide the syrup among 6 champagne flutes or trumpet-shaped glasses and drop 3 or 4 raspberries in each. Fill with the sparkling grape juice and serve.

campari pom fizz

Considered by many non-Italians to be an acquired taste, Campari bitters has been served as an aperitif in one form or another since it was invented in the 1860s. Made from a secret recipe of herbs, spices, fruits, and alcohol, its taste can be undeniably medicinal, so it is sometimes deliberately masked by ingredients like sweet vermouth in drinks such as the Americano or Negroni. Sanbittèr, an alcohol-free version of Campari, can pose the same challenge in creating a palatable aperitif that refreshes and stimulates without cloying the taste buds with added sweetness. The answer lies in the addition of sweet, yet tart, pomegranate syrup, for an aperitif that neither disguises nor overly exposes the uniqueness of the bitters, but instead blends beautifully to create a full-flavored refreshment. Sanbittèr, made by San Pellegrino, is available at many Italian and specialty markets, or you can order it online (see Resources).

SERVES 2

Ice

1 (3.4-ounce) bottle
Sanbittèr

2 tablespoons pomegranate
syrup

Splash of orange seltzer

2 orange slices, for garnish

Fill 2 old-fashioned glasses with ice. Divide the Sanbittèr and syrup between the glasses, add a splash of seltzer, then stir and serve garnished with an orange slice on each rim.

spiced sparkler

This uniquely delicious drink derives its flavor from an infusion of tantalizing spices that will surprise and delight your guests. Assertive star anise, cinnamon, and all-spice highlight the base syrup, which also has a floral hint from orange blossom water. A carbonated white grape juice provides the sparkle, although for guests who drink alcohol you may top off with the popular Italian Prosecco or a dry champagne. It makes a lovely prelude to a Middle Eastern meal and is particularly good as an accompaniment for nibbles such as spiced or glazed nuts.

SERVES 6

Spiced Syrup

³/₄ **cup water**

³/₄ **cup sugar**

2 whole star anise

1 cinnamon stick

¹/₂ **teaspoon whole allspice, cracked**

1 teaspoon orange blossom water

1 (750 ml) bottle no-sugar-added sparkling white grape juice, well chilled

To make the Spiced Syrup, combine the water and sugar in a small saucepan and bring to a boil, stirring often. When the sugar has dissolved, remove from the heat and add the spices. Cool the syrup to room temperature, then stir in the orange blossom water. Strain through a fine-mesh sieve into an airtight container and chill before using.

Divide the syrup among 6 champagne flutes and top with the sparkling juice.

my spanish cheri

As an accompaniment to tapas, the traditional drink of choice is a glass of dry sherry. Unlike sweet sherries and in the true style of an aperitif, a fine glass of dry sherry is delicate in flavor, pale in color, and subtly aromatic and can prepare the palate for the festivities to come. Some simple pantry ingredients come together surprisingly well in this mock sherry that will please even the pickiest aperitif aficionados. Serve with Marcona almonds, Manchego cheese, and membrillo (quince paste) for the perfect Spanish flair.

SERVES 4

1 cup no-sugar-added white grape juice

²/₃ cup spring water

¹/₂ cup cola

1 tablespoon sherry vinegar

Pour all of the ingredients into a small decanter and shake lightly to combine. Chill for 1 hour, then serve in sherry glasses.

pastiche pastis

When absinthe, the quintessential French aperitif, was banned in 1915 due to its supposed addictive and psychoactive properties (which later were proven to be non-existent), producers raced to find a suitable substitute. The result was pastis, an aniseed-based drink, usually served with a pitcher of cold spring water to dilute its intensity and create a characteristic milky appearance. Pastis, and drinks that include it, are enjoying a newfound popularity in the United States as a refreshing prelude to dinner. In this version, Ricard's alcohol-free Pacific pastis steps in with all of the essential flavor and none of the buzz, enhanced with an infusion of star anise and lemon served on the side for diluting. Serve with green Picholine olives, a thinly sliced baguette, and a dish of fruity olive oil with a pinch of herbes de Provence and fleur de sel for dipping.

=== SERVES 2

3 ounces Pacific pastis

1 ($^1/_2$-liter) bottle spring water, well chilled

2 whole star anise

$^1/_2$ lemon, thinly sliced

1 tablespoon superfine sugar, or more to taste

1 cup ice (optional)

Divide the pastis between 2 highball glasses.

Combine the spring water, star anise, lemon slices, and sugar in a glass pitcher, stir until the sugar dissolves, then add the ice if you wish. Use to dilute the Pacific pastis to taste.

black currant ratafia

Aromatic and flavorful, ratafias are classic Mediterranean aperitifs that are tradi-tionally made by infusing red wine with seasonal spices and fruit. In this buzz-free ratafia, black currant juice serves as the base, resulting in a hearty, somewhat sweet version that's perfect for serving hot during the winter holidays. A great alternative to mulled wine, it goes well with all types of cheeses and flat breads. Look for black currant juice in your supermarket or at an ethnic market. Clementines are a cross between a Seville orange and a tangerine, either of which could be used when cle-mentines are unavailable.

SERVES 6

1 (32-ounce) bottle black currant juice

1 clementine, quartered

1 bay leaf

1 cinnamon stick

1 teaspoon coriander seeds

$^1/_2$ teaspoon black peppercorns

$^1/_2$ teaspoon whole cloves

Combine all of the ingredients in a large sauce-pan and bring to a boil, then lower the heat and simmer for 5 minutes. Let the ratafia steep for 1 hour, then pour it through a fine-mesh sieve and discard the solids.

Reheat before serving in punch cups, or refriger-ate for up to 2 days, then reheat before serving.

note: At other times of the year, try substitut-ing pomegranate or cranberry juice for the black currant juice for a lighter interpretation that makes a refreshing start to any meal when served over ice.

ginger apple wassail

A warm aperitif can be a welcome respite on a cold evening before supper is served. Wassail, a drink that harks back to medieval times, was traditionally made with ale or hard cider, along with baked apples and toast. This alcohol-free version gets its foamy head from ginger beer, and small roasted apples provide a bit of whimsy. Serve with toast points dusted with cinnamon-sugar for utter authenticity.

SERVES 6

6 Lady apples

1 tablespoon sugar

$1/4$ teaspoon ground cinnamon

3 (12-ounce) bottles ginger beer

3 cups apple cider

Freshly ground nutmeg, for garnish

Preheat the oven to 375°F. Put the apples in a small roasting pan and sprinkle the sugar and cinnamon over them. Bake for about 35 minutes, until tender but still firm.

Whisk together the ginger beer and cider in a large saucepan over medium-low heat. Warm the mixture, but don't allow it to boil.

To serve, place an apple in each of 6 heatproof glass beer mugs, ladle in the wassail, and serve garnished with a dusting of nutmeg.

chapter 2

martinis and party cocktails

The days of making martinis strictly with gin and vermouth—either shaken or stirred—have given way to a more open-minded era with a multitude of renditions that purists deem dishonest but most everyone else finds delectably delightful. Many martinis are now made with flavored vodkas and any number of different mixers, from sour apple to chocolate, though all are still served in the classic cocktail glass, now known as a martini glass. This wide variety of flavors and twists lends itself more readily to alcohol-free versions, some that make use of prepared martini mixers, while others are created from the bottom up with innovative ingredients and garnishes.

Although stirringly popular, martinis are just one type of party cocktail that can be reinvented for nondrinkers. Cosmopolitans, manhattans, and mojitos are just a few of today's fashionable drinks that lend themselves to alcohol-free creativity. From tall, cool, and thirst quenching to neat and dramatic, the mocktails in this chapter will provide any host with a stunning repertoire of sober imbibements. When these dazzling drinks are served, whether at a casual get-together or a swanky cocktail party, no guest will be left out.

key lime mojito

The Cuban working class cocktail called the mojito has enjoyed recent popularity in U.S. bars and restaurants. Essentially a muddle of spearmint, lime, and sugar with a good dose of rum and a splash of club soda, this refreshing drink has served as the basis for a number of variations, from passion fruit to coconut. In this version, the traditional lime flavor is heightened by using the unique, petite Key lime, which boasts more intense acidity and bitterness and, of course, is the star of the popular dessert Key lime pie. Vanilla sugar adds an interesting layer of flavor that helps to balance the sour sensation. Fresh Key limes can be purchased in most supermarkets when in season, but in a pinch, bottled Key lime juice will fill in nicely, in which case you need not add the splash of spring water.

SERVES 1

3 Key limes, quartered (or 2 tablespoons Key lime juice)

1 tablespoon vanilla sugar

$^1/_4$ cup packed mint leaves

Splash of spring water

Crushed ice

Splash of lemon-lime soda

Key lime slice, for garnish

Mint sprig, for garnish

Put the quartered limes, sugar, mint leaves, and water in a mixing glass or cocktail shaker and muddle until the sugar is dissolved and a lime-mint syrup forms. Add ice and shake until well chilled. Strain into a highball glass half filled with crushed ice, top with the lemon-lime soda, and serve garnished with the lime slice and mint sprig.

caipirinha caprice

The caipirinha has recently begun to enjoy popularity outside of Brazil, where it is considered the national drink. Made with cachaça, *a sugarcane-based alcohol, the only other ingredients are usually sugar and lime. This version has an added bit of citrus from a muddle of lime, lemon, and orange (peels included), while ginger beer provides the kick. Look for muscovado or raw sugar cubes in the baking aisle of your supermarket and sugarcane swizzle sticks at specialty grocers or online.*

SERVES 1

¹/₂ lime, diced

¹/₂ small lemon, diced

¹/₂ small orange, diced

1 muscovado or raw sugar cube

Ginger beer

Crushed ice

Sugarcane swizzle stick, for garnish

Mint sprig, for garnish

Put the diced citrus in a mixing glass or cocktail shaker with the sugar cube. Add a splash of the ginger beer and muddle until the citrus juices are released. Strain into an old-fashioned glass filled with crushed ice and top off with the ginger beer. Garnish with the sugarcane swizzle stick and mint sprig.

mango rita

While others are sipping the real thing, here's an easy and delicious version you can make for nondrinkers using the same margarita mix you have on hand. This margarita is smooth and cool, and perfectly suited to any Mexican food you may be serving, so don't be surprised when it turns a few heads. Using a colorful salt to rim the glasses makes this mocktail especially festive.

SERVES 2

Lime wedge, for rimming

Colored coarse salt, for rimming

1 mango, peeled, seeded, and diced

1 cup crushed ice

1 cup prepared margarita mix

¹/₄ cup orange juice

2 mango slices, for garnish

Rub the lime wedge around the rims of 2 margarita glasses, then dip the rims of the glasses in the salt.

Combine the diced mango, ice, margarita mix, and orange juice in an electric blender and puree until smooth. Divide the mixture between the 2 rimmed glasses and serve garnished with the mango slices.

tweety bird

This refreshing take on the yellow bird cocktail makes use of bitter lemon soda to tone down the sweetness of the juices and lemon-lime soda. It's a terrific mocktail for a summer party and is an excellent alternative to margaritas for pairing with any Mexican or Latin type of hors d'oeuvres. You can combine the juices ahead of time, keep them chilled, and then add the sodas just before serving.

SERVES 4

½ cup orange juice, well chilled

½ cup white grapefruit juice, well chilled

½ cup pineapple juice, well chilled

1 cup lemon-lime soda, well chilled

½ cup bitter lemon soda, well chilled

4 pineapple wedges, for garnish

Pour the fruit juices into a small pitcher and stir to combine. Just before serving, stir in the lemon-lime and bitter lemon sodas, divide among 4 highball glasses, and serve garnished with the pineapple wedges.

fantasy island

When creamy tropical cocktails are on the menu, this fantastical buzz-free version will allow nondrinkers to join in the fun. Sweet and refreshing, the flavors of pineapple, grapefruit and coconut team up for an exotic smoothie type of drink. Frozen yogurt eliminates the need for ice in the blender while contributing another layer of flavor and texture. Experiment with substituting other tropical juices, such as guava or mango, for the pineapple and grapefruit juices to create a variety of tropical sensations.

SERVES 1

$1/2$ cup pineapple juice, well chilled

$1/2$ cup white grapefruit juice, well chilled

$1/4$ cup cream of coconut

1 cup vanilla frozen yogurt

Ice (optional)

Bite-size piece of fresh coconut, for garnish

Combine the juices, cream of coconut, and frozen yogurt in a blender and puree until smooth. Pour into a tumbler, with or without ice, and serve garnished with the fresh coconut on a cocktail pick.

coladatini

Meaning "strained pineapple" in Spanish, the piña colada lives up to its name in this cross between everyone's favorite island drink and a pineapple martini. The pure liquid essence of fresh pineapple combined with silky cream of coconut results in an ultrasmooth texture. Sweetly exotic with a faint fizz, this drink will elicit smiles of heavenly pleasure from your guests with every sip. Serve with a dish of macadamia nuts for added indulgence.

SERVES 1

1 cup fresh pineapple chunks

¹/₄ cup cream of coconut

Ice

Splash of orange seltzer

Pineapple spear, for garnish

Puree the pineapple in a food processor fitted with the steel blade until smooth and foamy. Strain into a cocktail shaker, add the cream of coconut and ice, and stir or shake until combined and well chilled.

Strain into a martini glass, add a splash of orange seltzer, stir, and serve garnished with the pineapple spear.

category 1 hurricane

The popular New Orleans cocktail gets downgraded to buzz free in this fruity cock-tail featuring passion fruit juice. Guava nectar adds another tropical dimension, and fresh lime juice helps balance the sweetness. Use Key lime juice if you can, for a unique flavor and a nod to the Florida Keys. Those who indulge in alcohol can add a shot or two of the usual rum if they like, but then you'll need to upgrade the category!

SERVES 1

¹/₂ cup passion fruit juice

¹/₂ cup guava nectar

¹/₄ cup orange juice

2 tablespoons freshly squeezed lime juice

1 tablespoon grenadine

Crushed ice

Splash of club soda

Orange slice, for garnish

Maraschino cherry, for garnish

Combine the passion fruit juice, guava nectar, orange juice, lime juice, and grenadine in a cocktail shaker. Add ice and shake until well combined. Strain into a hurricane or tulip-shaped glass half filled with crushed ice, add a splash of club soda, and serve garnished with the orange slice and cherry.

my mai tai dream

Trader Vic's Polynesian classic gets an alcohol-free makeover in this taste of the tropics that will whisk you away in a reverie of delight. You can easily find almond syrup in almost any store that carries flavored syrups for coffee, but it's worth tracking down French orgeat syrup for its superior almond flavor and aroma. Rose's Lime Juice provides some necessary tang to balance the sweetness of this cocktail. Freshly squeezed orange juice is a must, but the traditional umbrella garnish is purely optional!

SERVES 1

$^1/_2$ **cup freshly squeezed orange juice**

1 tablespoon Rose's Lime Juice

1 tablespoon orgeat or almond syrup

Crushed ice

Dash of grenadine

Splash of lemon-lime seltzer

Mint sprig or cocktail umbrella, for garnish

Combine the orange juice, Rose's Lime Juice, and syrup in a cocktail shaker. Add ice and shake until well combined. Strain into an old-fashioned glass half filled with crushed ice. Add a dash of grenadine and a splash of lemon-lime seltzer, stir, and serve garnished with the mint sprig or umbrella.

blushing virgin

The original blushing lady cocktail is a medley of sweet, sour, and tart, with a coura-geous shot of vodka. Here, she flaunts her delicious flavor combination but keeps the bold buzz at bay. Although mouth-puckering pomegranate, grapefruit, and lemon dominate, a sugar-rimmed glass adds a bit of sweetness to every sip, and red or pink rimming sugar will definitely add to her beauty. Although any grapefruit soda will work, look for Jamaican Ting, a grapefruit soda with terrific flavor that's available in many ethnic markets.

SERVES 1

Lemon wedge, for rimming

Coarse sugar, for rimming

Ice

¹/₄ cup no-sugar-added pomegranate juice

1 tablespoon freshly squeezed lemon juice

¹/₂ cup grapefruit soda

Lemon slice, for garnish

Rub the lemon wedge around the rim of an old-fashioned glass, then dip the rim of the glass in the sugar.

Fill the rimmed glass with ice. Add the pome-granate juice, lemon juice, and grapefruit soda, stir, and serve garnished with the lemon slice.

soft sea breeze

The refreshing tastes of grapefruit and cranberry find a home in this alcohol-free version of the popular sea breeze cocktail. Using pink grapefruit juice, rather than white, adds sweetness and color, while an unexpected hint of lime lends a further dimension. Although pink and Ruby Red grapefruit juices are readily available, freshly squeezed grapefruit juice will add a special touch. Serve with traditional salty nibbles, like mixed nuts or pretzels.

SERVES 4

2 cups pink or Ruby Red grapefruit juice, well chilled

2 cups cranberry juice, well chilled

Juice of 2 limes

Ice (optional)

1 (¹/₂-inch) slice pink grapefruit, quartered, for garnish

Pour the juices into a pitcher and stir to combine. Pour into 4 highball or juice glasses, with or without ice, and serve garnished with the quartered grapefruit slice.

tom collins's cousin

The gin-based Tom Collins is always a popular summer cocktail. Here, Tom's abstinent cousin takes center stage in a version that raises simple lemonade to new heights. Nothing is more thirst quenching than this tall, cool drink made with a hint of juniper berries, the ingredient that gives gin its unique flavor. Look for juniper berries in the spice aisle of your supermarket or gourmet grocer, or order them online. The traditional Collins garnish of an orange slice and red cherry gives way to a lemon slice and the unusual green maraschino.

SERVES 1

Ice

2 tablespoons freshly squeezed lemon juice

2 tablespoons spring water

¹/₄ teaspoon dried juniper berries, crushed

2 teaspoons superfine sugar

³/₄ cup club soda, well chilled

Lemon slice, for garnish

Green maraschino cherry, for garnish

Combine the ice, lemon juice, spring water, juniper berries, and sugar in a cocktail shaker and shake well to combine. Strain into a collins glass filled with ice, add the club soda, stir, and serve garnished with the lemon slice and cherry.

almond sour

Not too sweet and enhanced with the delicious flavor of almonds, this drink will delight abstinent guests who enjoy a hint of something different in a plain lemonade. Orgeat or almond syrup provides that something different, while a generous amount of mouth-puckering fresh lemon and lime juice keeps this drink from being syrupy sweet. Tart and refreshing, this mocktail is great for an outdoor summer party and goes well with all types of nibbles and hors d'oeuvres. Serve in wine goblets for a classy yet casual party presentation.

SERVES 1

Ice

1 tablespoon orgeat or almond syrup

1 tablespoon freshly squeezed lime juice

1 tablespoon freshly squeezed lemon juice

Lemonade

Fill a wineglass with ice cubes and pour in the syrup and juices. Top off with the lemonade, stir gently, and serve.

fizzy lime tonic

The classic British gin and tonic gets a sober makeover with this not-too-sweet, refreshing drink that's a perfect partner for a summertime picnic or barbecue. Alcohol-free Rose's Lime Juice serves as the base, while quinine, the dominant ingredient in tonic water, provides the bitter touch. A surprise dash of grenadine and a sprig of mint add a bit of unexpected flavor.

SERVES 1

Ice

1 tablespoon Rose's Lime Juice

1 cup tonic water

Dash of grenadine

Mint sprig, for garnish

Fill a highball glass with ice. Pour in the Rose's Lime Juice and tonic water, stir, then add the grenadine. Serve garnished with the mint sprig.

cosmopolitan charade

Deception never tasted so good! Fool them all as you sip from this alcohol-free version of a trendy cocktail that offers all of the taste and none of the alcohol. Use a festive martini glass, and frost it by placing it in the freezer for at least 30 minutes before pouring in the mocktail. Serve on its own or with traditional salty bar nibbles, like pretzels and peanuts.

SERVES 1

$^1/_2$ cup cranberry juice cocktail

$^1/_2$ cup no-sugar-added white grape juice

2 tablespoons Rose's Lime Juice

Ice

Splash of orange seltzer

Orange slice, for garnish

Combine the juices in a cocktail shaker, add some ice, and shake until combined and well chilled. Strain into a martini glass, add a splash of orange seltzer, stir, and serve garnished with the orange slice.

big apple tease

Inspired by the manhattan cocktail, which originated in none other than The Big Apple at the turn of the nineteenth century, this mock version comes close to teasing the palate into believing it's the real thing. Where most virgin manhattan recipes call for a primary mix of cranberry and orange juices, this mocktail starts off with a mock bourbon and builds from there. Cranberry juice and a small amount of juice from a jar of maraschino cherries fill in nicely for the sweet red vermouth, while a dash of lime juice and the classic cherry garnish complete the tease.

SERVES 1

¹/₃ cup Copycat Bourbon (see recipe below)

¹/₃ cup cranberry juice

1 tablespoon maraschino cherry juice

Dash of lime juice

Ice

Maraschino cherry, for garnish

Combine the Copycat Bourbon and juices in a cocktail shaker, add ice, and shake until combined and well chilled. Strain into an old-fashioned glass and serve garnished with the cherry.

copycat bourbon

1¹/₂ cups apple juice

¹/₄ cup dark, aged balsamic vinegar

¹/₄ cup white balsamic vinegar

1 teaspoon alcohol-free vanilla extract

Combine all of the ingredients in a pitcher, stir well, and chill until ready to use. Makes 1 pint, enough for 6 Big Apple Tease cocktails. Stored in the refrigerator in an airtight container, it will keep for 3 days.

cranberry razzletini

This dazzling faux martini is as lovely to look at as it is delicious to drink. Cranberry juice adds just enough tartness to counter the sweetness of the raspberry elements, and a hint of lime also contributes to the balance. Sparkling sugar and edible glitter are available at bakery supply shops, or you can order them online. Choose an elegant skewer for the raspberries to add to the razzle-dazzle of the presentation.

SERVES 1

3 or 4 raspberries, for garnish

Sparkling sugar or edible glitter, for garnish

1 tablespoon raspberry syrup

$^1/_2$ cup cranberry juice

Juice of $^1/_2$ lime

Ice

Splash of lemon-lime seltzer

To make the garnish, thread 3 or 4 raspberries onto a metal skewer and roll in sparkling sugar or sprinkle with edible glitter.

Combine the syrup, cranberry juice, and lime juice in a cocktail shaker. Add ice and shake until combined and well chilled. Strain into a martini glass, add a splash of lemon-lime seltzer, stir, and serve garnished with the sparkling raspberry skewer across the rim of the glass.

rosemary meyer lemon martini

Two coveted ingredients of the kitchen come together in this dry, sophisticated drink that's both tangy and aromatic: rosemary and Meyer lemon. Meyer lemons are less sour than a true lemon and have a hint of mandarin orange. You can use freshly squeezed juice or bottled. Serve in small martini glasses with a dish of herb-marinated olives and caperberries for nibbling.

SERVES 4

Rosemary Syrup

1 cup water

1 cup sugar

3 (4-inch) sprigs of
rosemary

1 cup Meyer lemon juice,
strained if freshly squeezed

Splash of spring water, or
more to taste

Ice

4 small sprigs of rosemary,
for garnish

To make the Rosemary Syrup, combine the water and sugar in a small saucepan and bring to a boil, stirring to dissolve the sugar. Add the rosemary sprigs, lower the heat, and simmer for 3 minutes. Cool the syrup to room temperature, then remove the rosemary, and chill before using.

Working in batches if necessary, combine the syrup, lemon juice, and spring water in a cocktail shaker. Add ice and shake until combined and well chilled. Strain into 4 martini glasses and serve garnished with the rosemary sprigs.

summer's rose martini

Two of summer's best offerings, watermelon and roses, are combined here to create a fragrant and refreshing mock martini perfect for sipping in the garden or on the patio. Rose water, a floral distillation used in many Middle Eastern dessert recipes, is completely alcohol-free, unlike most flavoring extracts. It's particularly potent, so use it with a light hand. Depending upon the sweetness of the watermelon, you may want to adjust the amount of sugar. Beautiful to behold and exotically flavored, this is the perfect drink to serve in lieu of those popular Midori-based martinis. Make sure you use roses grown for culinary use, or organic rose petals from your own garden.

SERVES 4

6 cups watermelon chunks, preferably seedless

1 tablespoon superfine sugar, or more to taste

1 teaspoon lemon juice

Pinch of sea salt

1 teaspoon rose water

Splash of lemon-lime seltzer

4 pink rose petals, for garnish

In a food processor fitted with the steel blade, combine the watermelon, sugar, lemon juice, and salt. Process until smooth, then pour through a fine-mesh sieve into a bowl, pressing on the solids to extract as much liquid as possible. Taste and add more sugar if need be, then stir in the rose water. Chill for at least 1 hour before serving, then divide among 4 martini glasses, add a splash of seltzer to each, and serve garnished with the rose petals.

granny's martini

Garnished with a slice of green Granny Smith apple, this easy mocktail makes use of prepared sour apple martini mix and a few clever additions to create a delicious buzz-free version of the popular appletini. Prepared cocktail mixes, which can be handy when time is of the essence, are readily available in the beverage aisle of most supermarkets. With its sparkle, flair, and crisp, fresh taste of apple, this mocktail is perfect for sipping alongside creamy French Brie and crackers.

SERVES 1

$^1/_2$ **cup sour apple martini mix, well chilled**

$^1/_2$ **cup sparkling apple juice, well chilled**

Splash of bitter lemon soda, or more to taste

Granny Smith apple slice, for garnish

Pour the martini mix into a large martini glass. Stir in the sparkling apple juice and bitter lemon soda, and serve garnished with the apple slice.

blackberry teani

Strong blackberry tea is the secret ingredient in this refreshing mock martini that will have guests clamoring for more. Make extra tea ahead of time and keep it chilled so you can quickly make seconds. Fresh blackberries on pretty drink skewers will finish your "teani" off in style. Serve alongside creamy goat cheese on crackers with a garnish of blackberry preserves, which will provide a good balance for the tea's tannins.

SERVES 1

1 cup boiling water

2 blackberry-flavored tea bags

2¹/₂ tablespoons blackberry syrup

Ice

Lemon twist, for garnish

Blackberries, for garnish

Pour the boiling water over the tea bags and steep for about 5 minutes, until dark and strong. Remove the tea bags and cool the tea to room temperature.

Combine the tea and syrup in a cocktail shaker, add ice, and stir or shake until combined and well chilled. Strain into a large martini glass and serve garnished with the lemon twist and blackberries.

passion fruitini

The musky flavor of passion fruit highlights this tempting mocktini that's perfect for a party featuring exotic fruity cocktails. Aromatically enticing, passion fruit is a native of South America, but the variety most commonly available these days, which is small and purple-skinned, is primarily grown in California. White cranberry juice adds a touch of flavor without interfering with the color, while a dash of bitters helps balance the sweetness. For a delicious pairing, serve these with crackers and creamy cheese spreads.

SERVES 1

¹/₂ cup passion fruit juice

¹/₄ cup white cranberry juice

Dash of blood orange bitters

Ice

1 teaspoon passion fruit seeds

Splash of lemon-lime seltzer

Combine the juices and bitters in a cocktail shaker, add ice, and shake until combined and well chilled. Strain into a martini glass, stir in the passion fruit seeds, and top with a splash of lemon-lime seltzer.

lychee nutini

Lychee nuts have a unique and intoxicating honey and floral aroma and flavor. Here the juice is featured in an alcohol-free martini with cranberry and apple juices for a superb cocktail with an exotic flair. Lychee juice can be found canned on its own, or with the fruit, at most Asian markets and some supermarkets. Although they can be hard to find, fresh lychee nuts have deep pink, prickly outer casings that make for an exciting cocktail garnish.

SERVES 1

¹/₄ **cup apple juice**

¹/₄ **cup cranberry juice**

¹/₄ **cup lychee juice**

1 tablespoon lime juice

Ice

Fresh or canned lychee nut, for garnish

Combine all of the juices in a cocktail shaker, add ice, and shake until combined and well chilled. Strain into a martini glass and serve garnished with a skewered lychee nut.

tuscan peppertini

Pepperoncini, also called Tuscan peppers, are small, slightly hot, banana-shaped members of the bell pepper family. Commonly found pickled and jarred, they're often used in sandwiches and salads. Here, they add a bit of heat and brininess, making for a great alternative to martinis made with pepper vodka. White cranberry juice, slightly sweet and less acidic than its red counterpart, provides the balance for the sea salt and brine, while blood orange bitters and a whole pepperoncini add subtle flavor and visual interest. Serve with crumbled Grana Padano or Parmigiano-Reggiano cheese and breadsticks for a delicious start to a Tuscan-themed evening.

SERVES 2

2 pepperoncini

Coarse sea salt, preferably Mediterranean

1¹/₃ cups white cranberry juice

2 teaspoons blood orange bitters

Ice

Splash of pepperoncini brine

Rub the pepperoncini around the rims of 2 martini glasses, then dip the rims of the glasses in the salt. Reserve the pepperoncini for garnish.

Combine the cranberry juice and bitters in a cocktail shaker, add ice, and stir or shake until combined and well chilled. Strain into the rimmed glasses, add a splash of brine to each, stir, and serve garnished with the reserved pepperoncini.

gingertini

Intensely flavored ginger tea provides the bite in this simple martini designed for ginger lovers. Bold in flavor, with a slightly sweet finish, this mocktail will awaken your taste buds with pleasure after each sip. Feel free to add an extra splash of ginger ale, however, if more sensitive palates need a bit of soothing. Serve as an accompaniment to sushi or California rolls.

SERVES 2

1 cup boiling water

2 ginger tea bags

2 tablespoons honey

Ice

Splash of ginger ale, or more to taste

2 chunks of crystallized ginger, for garnish

Pour the boiling water over the tea bags and steep for 5 minutes. Remove the tea bags and cool the tea to room temperature.

Pour the tea into a cocktail shaker, add the honey and ice, and shake until combined and well chilled. Strain into 2 martini glasses, add a splash of ginger ale to each, stir, and serve garnished with the crystallized ginger on cocktail picks.

elderflower martini

The fragrant blossoms of the elderberry shrub have long been a treasured flavoring for European cordials and liqueurs and now have finally found an audience in the United States. Reminiscent of honeysuckle with a hint of tartness, elderflowers are also used to make a sweet, alcohol-free syrup that's a popular addition to both soda water and champagne. Here, it stars in a refreshing martini with a supporting cast of lemon, lime, and white cranberry juice, making for a perfect summertime cocktail. Elderflower syrup is available at Ikea and some specialty grocers, or you can order it online. You may substitute elderflower liqueur in place of the syrup for guests who prefer a bit of alcohol.

SERVES 1

1 lemon twist

1 lime twist

1/2 cup white cranberry juice

1/4 cup freshly squeezed lime juice

2 tablespoons elderflower syrup

Ice

Splash of lemon-lime seltzer

Put the lemon and lime twists in a martini glass. Combine the white cranberry juice, lime juice, and syrup in a cocktail shaker and add the ice. Shake until combined and well chilled, then strain into the martini glass and top off with the seltzer.

hibiscus spritzer

Although more recently popular as a unique addition to cocktails in the form of liqueur, hibiscus flowers have long been a revered ingredient of herbal concoctions and teas. Here, a tangy tea blend combined with the syrup from the jar of hibiscus and the gorgeous flower itself come together to create an elegant drink fit for special occasions. A bit of bubbly, in the form of sparkling grape juice, creates a beautiful upward flow of fizz that appears to emanate from the hibiscus flower at the bottom of the flute. Look for hibiscus flowers in syrup at specialty food stores, or you can order them online.

SERVES 1

1 hibiscus flower in syrup

1 tablespoon hibiscus syrup

1 tablespoon strongly brewed rosehip or hibiscus blend tea, such as Celestial Seasonings Red Zinger, chilled

Sparkling white grape juice, preferably no-sugar-added, chilled

Place the hibiscus flower in the bottom of a large champagne flute. Stir together the syrup and tea in a small cup and pour the mixture over the flower. Top off with the sparkling white grape juice and serve immediately.

shampagne cocktail

A classic and elegant quaff created in the 1850s, the quintessential champagne cocktail can make any event celebratory. Simply composed of a sugar cube saturated with bitters (normally Angostura) and topped with champagne, this traditional cocktail lends itself quite easily to a mock version. Alcohol-free blood orange bitters saturates the sugar cube, and a not-too-sweet sparkling grape juice does the topping off. Using a twist of orange instead of the traditional twist of lemon will help guests tell their drinks apart from those that contain alcohol. This is the perfect nonalcoholic beverage for weddings and other events where toasting is required.

SERVES 1

1 sugar cube

Splash of blood orange bitters

Sparkling white grape juice, preferably no-sugar-added, chilled

Orange twist, for garnish

Drop the sugar cube into a champagne flute and add a good splash of bitters to saturate the sugar cube. Slowly pour in the sparkling grape juice and serve garnished with the orange twist.

chapter 3

mealtime libations

What you drink at mealtime can be almost as important as the meal itself. The perfect beverage can make good food taste great, while the wrong choice could leave your taste buds disappointed. Sommeliers know how to choose the perfect wine to complement the nuances of intricate flavors, and also can often recommend the ideal nonalcoholic drink to accompany any dish. Ideally, what you drink should enhance your dining experience without interfering with the flavors in any dish, be they bold or subtle.

Many alcohol-based drinks have become associated with specific foods because they complement one another so well. An assertive Cabernet with steak au poivre or an ice-cold lager with fish and chips are good examples. Some drinks that contain alcohol are typically paired with certain mealtimes, such as a mimosa or Bloody Mary with brunch. Creating the right alcohol-free cocktail to offer your guests with the food you're serving, whether it be at breakfast, lunch, or dinner, will not only add to their enjoyment of the meal, it will also make everyone who isn't drinking alcohol feel catered to and special.

mimosa sunrise

You'll never be left out of the brunch crowd again when you sip this alcohol-free version of a champagne standard with a nod to the classic tequila sunrise. A hint of apricot adds interest and depth, while syrupy grenadine rises from the bottom to create the vista. This is the perfect libation to accompany brunch, and is also a festive choice for daytime weddings and parties.

SERVES 1

$1/2$ **cup orange juice, preferably freshly squeezed, well chilled**

1 tablespoon apricot nectar, well chilled

1 teaspoon grenadine

$1/3$ **cup club soda, well chilled**

Maraschino cherry, for garnish

In a wine glass or champagne flute, stir together the orange juice and apricot nectar. Carefully and slowly drip the grenadine down the inside edge of the glass so it settles on the bottom. Top with the club soda, without stirring, and serve garnished with the cherry.

bananarama bliss

This delicious margarita alternative, which is ideal to serve at brunch, can be easily spiked with tequila for those guests who prefer a bit of alcohol. This creamy quaff is less sweet and dessertlike than a banana smoothie due to the addition of lime, making it more suitable as a drink to accompany food. Make sure the bananas are soft and ripe for maximum flavor, and look for coarse colored sugar crystals or sanding sugar to rim the glasses for a festive touch. Squeeze a little lime juice on the slices of banana for the garnish to keep them from browning.

SERVES 4

Lime wedge, for rimming

Coarse colored sugar, for rimming

1 (6-ounce) can frozen limeade concentrate

³/₄ cup spring water

¹/₂ cup orange juice

4 cups crushed ice

3 ripe bananas, peeled and sliced

4 lime slices, for garnish

4 banana slices, for garnish

Rub the lime wedge around the rims of 4 large margarita glasses, then dip the rims of the glasses in the sugar.

Working in batches if necessary, combine the frozen limeade, water, orange juice, and ice in an electric blender and puree until smooth. Add the 3 sliced bananas and continue blending until creamy. Pour into the rimmed glasses and serve garnished with the lime and banana slices.

breakfast bellini

The classic Bellini, created at Harry's Bar in Venice, Italy, is made from pureed white peaches and a good splash of Asti Spumante or Prosecco—light sparkling Italian wines that are akin to champagne. With its refreshing and lively flavor, this alcohol-free cousin is perfect for brunch entertaining. Sparkling white grape juice fills in for the wine, and a twist of lime adds a subtle interest and tang. When fresh white or yellow peaches are at their peak, use a fresh puree in place of the nectar.

SERVES 1

$^1/_4$ **cup peach nectar, well chilled**

$^1/_2$ **cup sparkling white grape juice, preferably no-sugar-added, well chilled**

Lime twist

Peach slice, for garnish

Pour the peach nectar into a champagne flute or juice glass, gently stir in the sparkling white grape juice, and serve garnished with the lime twist and peach slice.

fuzzy wuzzy

This is a creamy and delicious alcohol-free version of the cocktail known as the fuzzy navel, which is based on peach schnapps. Peach and apricot nectar, as well as a splash of orange seltzer and lime juice, come together to create a cocktail suitable for all ages and sure to please anyone who enjoys sweet and fruity drinks. It's ideal for serving at breakfast or brunch and delicious with croissants and muffins.

SERVES 1

$^1/_2$ **cup peach nectar**

$^1/_3$ **cup apricot nectar**

Ice

Splash of orange seltzer

Dash of Rose's Lime Juice

Orange slice, for garnish

Maraschino cherry, for garnish

Stir together the nectars in an old-fashioned glass, then add a few ice cubes. Add a splash of orange seltzer and a dash of lime juice, stir, and serve garnished with the orange slice and cherry.

bloody salsa maria

Jalapeños take the place of horseradish to provide the heat in this bold, buzz-free rendition of a morning tradition. Vegetable juice adds more flavor than the usual tomato juice, and the array of garden garnishes will be the envy of any celery-munching Bloody Mary drinkers who may be looking on. Adjust the heat level as desired by using your favorite prepared salsa—mild, medium, or hot. This is a terrific drink and appetizer all rolled into one!

SERVES 1

Cherry tomato, for garnish

Carrot round, for garnish

Pickled jalapeño slice, for garnish

Small radish, for garnish

Yellow bell pepper slice, for garnish

Ice

1 (6-ounce) can low-sodium vegetable juice, chilled

1 tablespoon prepared salsa, not chunky

1 teaspoon freshly squeezed lime juice

Pinch of celery salt

Pinch of ground cumin

Lime wedge, for garnish

Prepare the vegetable garnish by threading the cherry tomato, carrot, jalapeño, radish, and bell pepper on a bamboo skewer.

Put a few ice cubes in a tumbler. Add the vegetable juice, salsa, lime juice, celery salt, and cumin, and stir well to combine. Insert the skewer into the drink and garnish the rim of the glass with the lime wedge.

variation: Substitute cooked shrimp for the vegetables on the skewer for a unique brunch shrimp cocktail.

happy as a clam digger

Featuring the salty sea taste of Clamato juice, a delicious blend of tomato and clam juices, this buzz-free take on the traditional clam digger will delight all clam fans and beachcombers. Tabasco sauce provides the heat, while a surprise dose of carrot juice adds a subtle and unique layer of flavor. Serve with appetizers like clams or oysters on the half shell and garlicky breadsticks for the perfect seafaring venture.

SERVES 1

1 cup Clamato juice, or
$^1/_2$ cup tomato juice and
$^1/_2$ cup clam juice

$^1/_4$ cup carrot juice

1 teaspoon freshly
squeezed lemon juice

$^1/_8$ teaspoon Tabasco sauce

Dash of Worcestershire
sauce

Pinch of garlic salt

Ice

Long carrot stick, for
garnish

Lemon slice, for garnish

Combine the Clamato juice, carrot juice, lemon juice, Tabasco, Worcestershire sauce, and garlic salt in a cocktail shaker. Add ice and shake until combined and well chilled. Strain into a highball glass and serve garnished with the carrot stick and lemon slice.

dragon quencher

The aromatic herb tarragon, also called dragon's wort, provides subtle flavor in this creative answer to the classic vodka greyhound, made with vodka and grapefruit juice. Anise-scented tarragon syrup combines beautifully with the sour component of grapefruit to create a refreshing drink suitable for dishes with a light herb seasoning, particularly fish. Grapefruit bitters, like Angostura bitters, contain a small amount of alcohol, so if guests strictly abstain from alcohol, use blood orange bitters instead.

SERVES 4

Tarragon Syrup

¹/₂ **cup water**

¹/₂ **cup sugar**

2 (4-inch) sprigs of tarragon

Ice

3 cups white grapefruit juice, preferably freshly squeezed

Dash of grapefruit bitters or blood orange bitters

4 sprigs of tarragon, for garnish

To make the Tarragon Syrup, combine the water and sugar in a small saucepan and bring to a boil, stirring to dissolve the sugar. Add the tarragon sprigs, lower the heat, and simmer for 3 minutes. Cool the syrup to room temperature, then remove the tarragon, and chill before using.

Fill 4 highball glasses with ice and divide the syrup and grapefruit juice among them. Add a dash of bitters to each, stir to combine, and serve garnished with the tarragon sprigs.

pomegranate lassi

Yogurt-based lassi drinks are a popular offering at Indian restaurants. Not overly sweet, they're wonderfully soothing to the palate and are an ideal beverage to accompany a spicy dish, such as a curry. Mango is the fruit most commonly used in these drinks, but in this recipe deliciously tart pomegranate yields a uniquely flavorful drink. It's a great alternative to creamy piña coladas, especially if you want something less sweet. Those who drink alcohol can add a shot of pomegranate liqueur if they wish.

SERVES 1

Thin kiwi slice, for garnish

Thin mango slice, for garnish

2 raspberries, for garnish

1 cup plain low-fat yogurt

2 tablespoons no-sugar-added pomegranate juice

2 tablespoons pomegranate syrup

Pinch of salt

Ice

To make the garnish, thread the kiwi, mango, and raspberries onto a skewer.

Combine the yogurt, juice, syrup, and salt in a blender and puree until smooth. Pour into a highball glass half filled with ice and place the skewer across the glass rim before serving.

icy spicy chai

Chai, meaning "tea" in many parts of the Eastern world but now familiarly thought of as spiced milk tea in the West, is easily prepared at home with delicious results. Icy and fragrant with hints of spice and maple, this wonderful picnic or afternoon beverage will please thirsty nondrinking guests who crave a change of pace from the usual iced tea offerings. You can double or triple the recipe as needed and even make it several days ahead. It's particularly good with Middle Eastern fare and aromatic rice dishes like biryani.

SERVES 2

1¹/₂ cups water

²/₃ cup whole milk or 2 percent milk

1 small cinnamon stick

8 cardamom pods, lightly crushed

4 whole cloves

1 (¹/₂-inch) piece fresh gingerroot, peeled and coarsely chopped

6 black peppercorns

2 black tea bags (regular or decaf)

2 tablespoons pure maple syrup, or more to taste

Ice

2 long cinnamon sticks, for garnish

Combine the water, milk, small cinnamon stick, cardamom, cloves, ginger, and peppercorns in a saucepan and bring just to a boil, stirring occasionally. Lower the heat and simmer for 5 minutes, then remove from the heat, add the tea bags, and steep for 6 to 8 minutes. Strain through a fine-mesh sieve into a small pitcher, stir in the maple syrup, and refrigerate until well chilled.

To serve, pour the chai into 2 ice-filled tumblers and garnish each with a long cinnamon stick.

tangerine blues

Here's a psychedelic drink for citrus lovers and those who like a colorful cocktail. It's suitable for children and also serves as a good alternative to cocktails based on orange juice, such as the tequila sunrise or screwdriver. Tangerine juice, with its bright hue and intense flavor, is now readily available in the juice section of many supermarkets, so you need not squeeze your own. If Murcott or honey tangerines are available, however, you may want to juice them so you can treat yourself to their unique fragrance and flavor. Monin's alcohol-free blue curaçao syrup has the same sweet yet bitter orange flavor of regular curaçao. However, you can also substitute the liquid from the blue maraschino cherry jar if you can't find blue curaçao syrup or if you're making this for kids or anyone who prefers a sweeter taste.

SERVES 1

³/₄ **cup tangerine juice, well chilled**

1 tablespoon blue curaçao syrup

Blue maraschino cherry, for garnish

Pour the juice into a clear highball or juice glass. Carefully and slowly drip the syrup down the inside edge of the glass so it settles on the bottom. Do not stir. Serve garnished with the blue cherry pierced with a cocktail pick.

blue raspberry lemonade

Colorful and tart, this lemonade gets its blue hue from Rose's Blue Raspberry cock-tail mix, which is available in many supermarkets. Limonata, a tart and fizzy Ital-ian lemon soda, provides the right balance and a touch of fizz, which everyday lemonade wouldn't do, so don't substitute unless you absolutely must. This is a great drink for barbecues and outdoor picnics where others may be sipping blue martinis or other eye-catching cocktails. Crushed ice will keep this cold and slushy, perfect for quenching any thirst.

SERVES 1

Crushed ice

¹/₄ cup Rose's Blue Raspberry cocktail mix

1 (6.75-ounce) bottle Limonata

Lemon slice, for garnish

Mound the crushed ice halfway up a tumbler. Pour the blue raspberry cocktail mix over the ice and top with the Limonata. Garnish the rim of the glass with a lemon slice and serve with a straw.

lavender soda

Recently, microbrewed sodas with unusual flavors have become popular. You can easily make your own by creating a flavored simple syrup and adding seltzer. Here, fragrant lavender takes center stage to create a light and summery soda fit for an afternoon of leisurely sipping. Dried culinary lavender is specifically designed for kitchen duty, having been grown without chemicals and produced without additives. If you have organically grown lavender in your own garden, you can certainly use that. Serve with shortbread or tea biscuits for a delightful pairing.

SERVES 4

Lavender Syrup

1 cup water

1 cup sugar

3 tablespoons dried culinary lavender, or 2 tablespoons fresh lavender florets

1 cup freshly squeezed lemon juice

Ice

Seltzer water

4 sprigs of dried culinary lavender, for garnish

To make the Lavender Syrup, combine the water and sugar in a small saucepan and bring to a boil, stirring to dissolve the sugar. Add the lavender, remove from the heat, and steep for 15 minutes. Strain through a fine-mesh sieve into an airtight container and chill before using.

Divide the syrup and lemon juice among 4 ice-filled tumblers and stir to combine. Top off each glass with seltzer water and serve garnished with the lavender sprigs.

ginger beer shandy

A cross between a traditional British shandy, made with beer and lemonade, and the Caribbean version, consisting of beer and ginger ale, this mug of cold suds with a true bite will delight any fan of cold beer. Keep frosted mugs handy and your ginger beer and lemonade well chilled to optimize the refreshing quality of this beverage, which is suitable for sipping (or gulping!) with bar food or snacks.

SERVES 1

1 cup lemonade, ice-cold

1 cup ginger beer, ice-cold

Pour the lemonade into a frosted pint-size beer mug. Top with the ginger beer and serve immediately.

note: If small amounts of alcohol aren't an issue, you can substitute dealcoholized beer (which contains 0.5 percent alcohol by volume) for the ginger beer, and replace half of the lemonade with ginger ale.

white tea fusion

This refreshing summer alternative to white wine is a great beverage to serve with a light lunch. Delicate yet aromatic white tea blends well with subtle fruit and herb flavors, such as the fennel and orange blossom used here. A smidgeon of honey adds just the right touch of sweetness, while a floral garnish provides color and elegance.

SERVES 2

2 cups boiling water

4 white tea bags

$^1/_4$ teaspoon fennel seeds

1 teaspoon orange blossom water

1 tablespoon orange blossom honey, or more to taste

Ice

2 edible flowers, for garnish

Pour the boiling water over the tea bags and steep for 6 minutes. Remove the tea bags, add the fennel seeds and orange blossom water, and infuse for 2 minutes. Strain into a small pitcher, then stir in the honey. Cool the tea to room temperature, then chill before using.

Divide the tea between 2 large wineglasses with a little ice and serve garnished with the flowers floating on top.

green tea cocktail

Iced green tea is elevated to a sophisticated quaff in this terrific alternative to a meal-enhancing white wine. Subtly flavored with a good balance of acidity and sweetness, it won't interfere with the delicate flavors of fish and seafood dishes. Healthy as well as refreshing to the palate, green tea offers abundant antioxidants while containing far fewer mouth-puckering tannins than black tea. Serve well chilled without adding ice, to prevent its subtle flavor from becoming diluted.

SERVES 4

1 cup boiling water

2 green tea bags

2 cups no-sugar-added white grape juice

1 tablespoon freshly squeezed lemon juice

1 cup ginger ale, well chilled

Pour the boiling water over the tea bags and steep for about 5 minutes, until strong and dark. Remove the tea bags and cool the tea to room temperature.

Combine the tea, grape juice, and lemon juice in a small pitcher and refrigerate until well chilled. To serve, divide among 4 wineglasses and top off each with ¼ cup of the ginger ale.

aussie soave

Refreshing and crisp like its namesake wine, this slightly sweet and effervescent copycat is perfect for serving on its own or with a light lunch or supper. Clean-tasting white cranberry juice infused with lemon and golden kiwi offers tart yet tantalizing layers of flavor. Gold kiwifruit have yellow flesh and are slightly sweeter and less acidic than their more common green-fleshed counterparts. They're available in many supermarkets. Serve this well chilled but not over ice, which would dilute the flavor, and top off with the seltzer just before serving.

SERVES 2

2¹/₂ cups white cranberry juice

¹/₂ cup no-sugar-added white grape juice

¹/₂ lemon, sliced

1 gold kiwifruit, peeled and coarsely chopped

Splash of lemon seltzer, well chilled

2 slices gold kiwifruit, for garnish

2 lemon twists, for garnish

Combine the cranberry and grape juices in a small pitcher. Add the lemon slices and chopped kiwi and refrigerate for at least 2 hours. Remove the fruit with a slotted spoon and discard it. Fill 2 wineglasses halfway with the juice mixture, top off each with a splash of lemon seltzer, and serve garnished with the kiwi slice and lemon twist.

dry grape grigio

Though its ingredients are simple, this wine alternative based on white grapes will pair well with most dishes, especially poultry. The grapefruit juice adds a pleasant acidity, and the dash of grenadine provides a hint of color and perks up the flavor. You can make enough for the dinner table ahead of time and keep it well chilled in a pitcher or decanter for serving. Try making this with red grape juice as well, for a good alternative to light red wine.

SERVES 4

3 cups no-sugar-added white grape juice

1 cup freshly squeezed white grapefruit juice, strained

Dash of grenadine

Stir or swirl all of the ingredients together in a pitcher or decanter. Chill before serving in white-wine glasses.

strawberry white sangria

America first tasted sangria at the 1964 World's Fair in New York and has been in Spanish heaven ever since. Although a multitude of variations exist, red wine—or sometimes white wine—is almost always the main ingredient. Here, a base of white grape juice is enlivened with the fresh flavor of juicy strawberries. Chilling overnight, if possible, will enhance its fragrance and color.

SERVES 4

1 quart no-sugar-added white grape juice

1 tablespoon freshly squeezed lemon juice

1 tablespoon blood orange bitters

1 pound strawberries, washed, hulled, and sliced

Ice

4 kiwi slices, for garnish

Combine the grape juice, lemon juice, and bitters in a pitcher and stir well. Add the strawberries and refrigerate for at least 4 hours, or preferably overnight. Pour into 4 ice-filled wine-glasses or punch cups and serve garnished with the kiwi slices.

note: If small amounts of alcohol aren't an issue, you can substitute dealcoholized wine (which contains 0.5 percent alcohol by volume) for the grape juice.

cranberry orange sangria

Refreshingly tart with a delightful orange twist, this alcohol-free answer to traditional sangria is perfect for pitchers or punch bowls. Have all of the juices well chilled and be sure to allow the fresh fruit flavor to infuse into the cranberry juice before adding the remaining ingredients. Delicious to sip at picnics, barbecues, and casual outdoor get-togethers, this fresh and crisp-tasting sangria goes down particularly well with classic paella or grilled seafood.

SERVES 8

1 lemon, sliced and seeded

1 orange, sliced and seeded

$^1/_2$ cup red seedless grapes, halved

$^1/_2$ cup green seedless grapes, halved

4 cups no-sugar-added cranberry juice, well chilled

2 cups cran-grape juice, well chilled

2 cups freshly squeezed orange juice, well chilled

$^1/_4$ cup lime juice

Ice

Put the fresh fruit in a large pitcher and pour the cranberry juice over it, then chill for 2 hours. Stir in the cran-grape juice, orange juice, and lime juice, add ice, and serve in wineglasses or punch cups.

pom zingfandel

The uniquely delicious flavor of pomegranate hooks up with the zing of lemon in this fizzy drink, making a nice accompaniment to almost any meal. Naturally sweet yet tart, and refreshing to the taste buds, it's a great stand-in when others may be sipping a Zinfandel or rosé. A hint of the vine from a muddling of red grapes rounds out the flavor, and a splash of seltzer provides some fizzy interest. It's especially delicious with a menu that features meat that isn't particularly lean, such as brisket or sausages.

SERVES 1

3 or 4 red grapes

1 teaspoon freshly squeezed lemon juice

Pinch of sugar

$^1/_4$ cup no-sugar-added pomegranate juice

Ice

$^1/_4$ cup seltzer water, well chilled

Combine the grapes, lemon juice, and sugar in a mixing glass or cocktail shaker and muddle until the grapes are broken down and have released their juices. Add the pomegranate juice and ice, and shake until combined and well chilled. Strain into a wineglass and top off with the seltzer.

red rooibos rioja

Rooibos, meaning "red bush," is a plant native to South Africa that's used to make herbal tea. Its high levels of antioxidants and its somewhat sweet, nutty flavor have contributed to its recent popularity. Nearly all tea manufacturers now make some type of rooibos tea, sometimes flavored with other herbs or fruit. Look for the plain rooibos so as not to interfere with the complexity of flavors in this recipe. Delicious on its own as an iced tea, here rooibos combines with a medley of bold fruit juices and a hint of pepper and vanilla to replicate the characteristics of Spanish Rioja wines. This makes a wonderful accompaniment to beef and other hearty meals.

SERVES 2

1 cup boiling water

1 rooibos tea bag

1 teaspoon black peppercorns

¹/₂ vanilla bean

1 cup no-sugar-added black cherry juice

1¹/₂ cupss no-sugar-added red grape juice

¹/₂ cup spring water

Pour the boiling water into a saucepan, add the tea bags, peppercorns, and vanilla bean, and steep for 10 minutes. Strain into a small pitcher or decanter and cool the tea to room temperature.

Add the juices and water and stir or swirl to combine. Serve in wineglasses at room temperature or slightly chilled.

cerise **noir**

The deep fruitiness of black currant and cherry, reminiscent of a Pinot Noir wine, are the distinctive flavors in this copycat drink perfect for any dinner menu. Muddled Bing cherries contribute their unique essence, while black currant tea provides a bit of necessary bite. This delicious alternative to iced tea or fruity drinks offers abstainers a delightful dose of sophistication and a depth of flavor normally found only in wine.

SERVES 1

5 Bing cherries, stems removed

¹/₃ cup strongly brewed black currant tea, chilled

¹/₃ cup black currant juice

¹/₃ cup no-sugar-added black cherry juice

Ice

Splash of orange seltzer

Orange twist, for garnish

Combine the cherries and tea in a mixing glass or cocktail shaker and muddle until the cherries are broken down and have released their juices. Add the black currant juice, cherry juice, and ice, and shake until combined and well chilled. Strain into a wineglass, add a splash of orange seltzer, and serve garnished with the orange twist.

açai iced tea

Açai, a small, dark purple berry that grows in tropical rain forests, has been called the world's healthiest fruit because of its impressive antioxidant content. Açai juice, available plain or in combination with other fruit juices, ranks healthier than pomegranate juice and even red wine when it comes to fighting free radicals. And when combined with tea, the result is not only a great alternative to heart-healthy red wine, but also the perfect taste to complement any meal. The combination of the tannins in tea and the slight tartness of the açai berries mimics the astringency of wine and refreshes the palate with every sip. Look for açai juice in the produce section or with refrigerated beverages.

SERVES 2

1 cup boiling water

1 orange pekoe tea bag

¹/₂ cup cold water

1 cup açai juice

Pour the boiling water over the tea bag and steep for 5 minutes. Remove the tea bag, add the cold water, and cool the tea to room temperature.

Combine the tea and açai juice in a small pitcher and refrigerate until well chilled. Serve in wineglasses.

chapter 4

dessert drinks

Serving a special drink with the final course of your meal can turn a simple dish into a lavish offering. Matching desserts—sorbets, cakes, or even just cookies—with an appropriate beverage that enhances their flavors will provide a celebratory conclusion to the meal. For those who drink alcohol, the possibilities are endless, from liqueur-spiked coffees to strong, syrupy cordials to classic endings such as a sauterne wine or ruby port. When choosing an alcohol-free match, the same rules apply as for imbibers: each sip should complement and balance each bite and contribute to diners' ultimate enjoyment of your dessert course.

Sometimes a dessert drink is so luxuriously rich or spectacularly presented that it can serve as the dessert itself. A dark chocolate martini with whipped cream or a fruity frappé of summer fruits may be all that's required for a perfect ending. Similarly, after a generous and sumptuous meal that has guests proclaiming there's no room for dessert, often just a little something sweet in a glass, instead of on a plate, will provide the ideal finish people may be craving but can't imagine consuming. No matter what the circumstances, one thing's for sure: offering the perfect drink to conclude the meal is bound to win you praise, if not sweet adoration.

hopscotch eggnog

While others enjoy a shot of whiskey in their seasonal eggnog, teetotalers and children can partake in the celebration with this deliciously rich and sweet drink. Homemade eggnog is a true luxury, but if you're pressed for time or are reluctant to serve anything containing raw eggs, feel free to substitute a ready-made version. Use a clear butterscotch syrup, such as those made for flavoring coffee, to mix with the eggnog and a caramel-colored sundae-type syrup for the garnish. Those who drink alcohol can use a splash of butterscotch schnapps instead of the syrup garnish.

SERVES 6

Homemade Eggnog

3 large egg yolks

$^1/_2$ cup superfine sugar

$^1/_2$ cup whole milk

1 cup heavy whipping cream

$^1/_2$ teaspoon alcohol-free vanilla extract

2 tablespoons clear butterscotch syrup

Pinch of nutmeg

Butterscotch sundae syrup, for drizzling

To make the eggnog, beat the egg yolks until light and fluffy in a large bowl using an electric mixer on medium-high speed. Add the sugar and continue beating until thick. Whisk in the milk and refrigerate for at least 3 hours, or overnight.

Within 1 hour before serving, beat the whipping cream and vanilla using an electric mixer on high speed until soft peaks form. Gently fold the whipped cream into the egg yolk mixture and keep chilled.

To serve, gently stir in the butterscotch syrup and nutmeg. Ladle into punch cups or old-fashioned glasses and drizzle the sundae syrup decoratively over the top.

note: As with all recipes containing raw egg, don't serve this to the young, the elderly, or pregnant or nursing moms.

toasted almond cordial

Opulently rich and flavorful, this softly sweet after-dinner drink will compete with any cream liqueur for a terrific finish to a meal. The wonderful and intoxicating aroma of almonds will hit people first as they lift their glass to sip. And when its velvety texture meets their lips, nondrinkers will swear this beverage must be taboo. If you're serving it straight up, you can use half-and-half, but if you're serving it over ice, make it with heavy cream so it can hold its own when the ice begins to melt. A couple of amaretti—Italian almond-flavored cookies—would make a fine accompaniment.

SERVES 4

1 tablespoon orgeat or almond syrup

1 cup half-and-half or heavy cream

4 small amaretti, slightly crushed

Ice, for serving (optional)

Combine all of the ingredients in a blender and puree until smooth. Keep chilled until ready to serve. Pour into 4 cordial glasses, or serve over ice in 4 highball glasses.

blood orange cordial

The blood orange, a variety of orange with crimson-colored flesh that usually hails from either Sicily or Spain, has become a popular citrus fruit in the kitchen and at the bar. Sweet yet bitter, with decidedly less acid than regular oranges, they appear in everything from savory sauces to sorbets. Here, a simple Blood Orange Syrup is the base for an alcohol-free cordial that can compete with Grand Marnier and Cointreau. Make the syrup ahead and keep it chilled in the refrigerator for up to 3 weeks.

SERVES 8

Blood Orange Syrup

1 cup blood orange juice

1 cup spring water

1 cup sugar

1 blood orange, thinly sliced

¹/₂ cup spring water

Dash of blood orange bitters

Ice (optional)

To make the Blood Orange Syrup, combine the blood orange juice, 1 cup spring water, and sugar in a saucepan. Bring to a simmer over medium heat, stirring often, until the sugar has dissolved. Add the blood orange slices, lower the heat, and continue to simmer until slightly thickened, about 10 minutes. Cool the syrup to room temperature, then remove and discard the orange slices and chill the syrup before using.

Just before serving, stir in the ¹/₂ cup spring water and bitters. Divide among 8 ice-filled old-fashioned glasses, or chill thoroughly and serve straight up.

banana split martini

Can't decide between dessert and drinks? How about imbibing one of America's favorite ice cream creations in sophisticated martini style? This rich and creamy treat with the flavor of fresh, ripe bananas and a drizzle of chocolate sundae syrup will delight all aficionados of ice cream parlors, and you'll receive oohs and aahs in the presentation department, as well. Serve in the largest martini glasses you can find.

SERVES 2

4 ('/2 cup) scoops vanilla ice cream

1 large, ripe banana, peeled and sliced

1 cup milk

Chocolate sundae syrup, for drizzling

Sweetened whipped cream, for garnish (page 7)

2 maraschino cherries, for garnish

Combine the ice cream, banana slices, and milk in a blender and puree until smooth. Drizzle the chocolate syrup over the inside of 2 large martini glasses, tilting and turning to coat. Divide the banana mixture between the glasses, and serve garnished with the whipped cream and cherries.

papaya passion

Tropical drink fans will love this layered mocktail that's dessert and drink all wrapped into one. Sweet, ripe papaya forms the bottom layer, followed by cream of coconut, then papaya juice, then a topping of decadent whipped cream. Look for yellow-skinned papayas that give slightly when pressed. When cut, the pulp should be soft and light orange in color. For those who prefer a little buzz with their passion, you can substitute crème de coconut liqueur for the cream of coconut.

SERVES 2

1 cup papaya chunks

1 teaspoon lime juice

1 teaspoon honey

2 tablespoons crushed ice

$1/2$ cup cream of coconut

$1/2$ cup papaya juice

2 tablespoons lightly sweetened whipped cream (page 7)

Combine the papaya chunks, lime juice, honey, and ice in a blender and puree until smooth. Divide between 2 champagne flutes. Carefully pour half of the cream of coconut on top of each layer of papaya, then carefully pour half of the papaya juice on top of each layer of cream of coconut. Top each flute with a tablespoon of whipped cream and serve with a long iced tea spoon.

falooda float

This unusual dessert drink, beloved in India and Pakistan, is fragrant with the heavenly scent of roses and garnished with takmaria *seeds (basil seeds) and strands of* falooda sev *(a type of vermicelli). It makes the perfect ending for a curry-based meal, and it's quite easy to make once you track down the unusual ingredients, which are usually available at Indian or Asian markets. The prepared* falooda *mixture can also be made into a delicious frozen dessert by freezing it in an ice cream maker.*

SERVES 2

2 cups whole milk

2 tablespoons superfine sugar

Pinch of ground cardamom

$^1/_4$ cup rose syrup

$^1/_2$ teaspoon *takmaria* seeds (basil seeds)

$^1/_4$ cup *falooda sev* or vermicelli noodles cut into 1-inch pieces

$^1/_2$ cup vanilla ice cream, plus 2 scoops for serving

1 tablespoon chopped pistachios, for garnish

Bring the milk to a boil, then remove from the heat, whisk in the sugar, cardamom, and syrup, and cool slightly before transferring to the refrigerator to chill completely.

Meanwhile, soak the *takmaria* seeds in a small bowl of water for 30 minutes, then drain and set aside. While the seeds are soaking, cook the *falooda sev* in boiling water for 3 minutes, then remove from the heat and let sit in its cooking water for 5 minutes. Drain the noodles, then run them under cold water to cool.

When the milk mixture is chilled, stir in the drained *falooda sev* and *takmaria* seeds. Add the $^1/_2$ cup ice cream and stir until just melted.

To serve, place a scoop of vanilla ice cream in each of 2 parfait glasses or tumblers, then ladle the *falooda* mixture over the ice cream. Garnish with the pistachios and serve with a straw and a long-handled spoon.

in the pink

Bubbly drinks such as pink champagne or Asti Spumante often make an appearance with dessert, especially at special celebrations like birthdays and anniversaries when cake is served. Keep this recipe on hand for occasions when nondrinkers need an equally special drink for toasting and sipping. If a number of abstinent guests will be partaking, you can make a large quantity of the basic mixture ahead of time, but wait to add the soda until just before serving so it doesn't lose its fizz.

SERVES 1

¹/₄ cup cranberry juice, well chilled

¹/₄ cup apple juice, well chilled

Splash of pulp-free orange juice, well chilled

Lemon-lime soda, well chilled

Combine the juices in a wine glass or champagne flute. Just before serving, top off with the lemon-lime soda.

strawberry watermelon slushy

Like a drinkable Italian ice, this refreshing dessert beverage offers the perfect con-
clusion to any meal on a hot summer day, or you can sip it for a welcome respite
from the heat between meals. Slushies containing alcohol, like the cosmopolitan
slushy, have enjoyed a recent surge in popularity, although rum-based slushies and
the renowned frozen margarita have certainly been around for quite some time.
Because this version doesn't contain alcohol, it will freeze up rather quickly, so it's
best to prepare it only a little bit ahead of time, if not on the spot. To help keep it
cold, chill the glasses in advance.

SERVES 1

1 cup cubed seedless
watermelon

1 cup strawberries, hulled
and halved

2 tablespoons superfine
sugar

1 tablespoon freshly
squeezed lemon juice

1 cup crushed ice

Small watermelon wedge,
for garnish

Combine the cubed watermelon, halved strawberries, sugar, and lemon juice in a blender and
puree until smooth. Gradually add the ice and
blend until the drink has a slushy consistency.
Pour into a chilled glass and serve garnished
with the watermelon wedge.

something blue

When searching for that "something blue" for nuptial celebrations, look no further than this delightfully delicious and elegant drink. Blue curaçao syrup lends its hue to a pineapple sorbet, which is served up in a champagne flute with sparkling juice. Because it doesn't contain alcohol, the sorbet will be decidedly hard when frozen, so be sure to take it out of the freezer a few minutes ahead of time to soften up. A dash of blood orange bitters ties the flavors of the sorbet and bubbly together just like a perfect marriage.

SERVES 1

¹/₂ cup sparkling white grape juice, preferably no sugar added, well chilled

Dash of blood orange bitters

1 small scoop Something Blue Sorbet (see recipe below)

Pour the sparkling grape juice into a champagne flute and add a dash of bitters. Carefully place the scoop of Something Blue Sorbet on top and serve.

something blue sorbet

1 cup water

1 cup sugar

1¹/₂ cups pineapple juice

¹/₂ cup blue curaçao syrup

1 tablespoon lime juice

Combine the water and sugar in a saucepan and bring to a boil, stirring until the sugar dissolves. Remove from the heat, stir in the pineapple juice, syrup, and lime juice, and chill for 2 to 3 hours in the refrigerator. Freeze the liquid in an ice cream maker according to the manufacturer's instructions, then transfer to an airtight container and freeze until ready to serve. Makes about 2 cups.

the lemon chiffon

This light, lemony dessert drink offers just the right balance of tart and sweet to finish a meal in fine style. Smooth and creamy Italian gelato is the ice cream of choice here, while homemade lemon syrup takes the place of limoncello liqueur. Serve this treat in old-time champagne coupes or saucer glasses if you have them. The candied lemon tops it off in inimitable style.

SERVES 2

2 small scoops vanilla gelato

1¹/₂ tablespoons Lemon Syrup (page 20)

Lightly sweetened whipped cream, for garnish (page 7)

2 Candied Lemon Slices (see recipe below), for garnish

---

1 lemon, thinly sliced and seeded

1 cup Lemon Syrup (page 20)

Chill a stainless steel bowl in the freezer for 15 minutes. Add the gelato and syrup, and whisk together until smooth and slightly frothy. Divide between 2 champagne coupes or martini glasses and serve garnished with a small dollop of whipped cream in the center and the candied lemon.

candied lemon slices

Put the lemon slices in a saucepan, add water to cover, and bring to a boil. Lower the heat and simmer for 5 minutes. Transfer the slices to a paper towel and discard the water. In a sauté pan wide enough to hold all of the slices in one layer, heat the syrup until very hot, but don't allow it to boil. Add the slices, remove from the heat, cover, and cool to room temperature. Transfer the lemon slices and syrup to an airtight container and refrigerate overnight. The lemon slices and their syrup will keep for up to 1 month in the refrigerator.

new york strawberry cheesecake

For those who would rather drink their dessert than eat it, here's a scrumptious concoction featuring the flavors of a decadent New York cheesecake. Like its namesake, this rich and creamy cocktail will amaze guests with its authentic flavor. The secret lies in the addition of cheesecake-flavored pudding mix, which is readily available in supermarkets. Try topping this libation with other popular cheesecake enhancements, such as blueberries or cherries.

SERVES 2

Graham cracker crumbs, for rimming

1 cup half-and-half

4 teaspoons cheesecake pudding mix

Dash of alcohol-free vanilla extract

Ice

2 tablespoons diced strawberries

2 teaspoons strawberry syrup

2 sprigs of mint, for garnish

Lightly moisten the rims of 2 martini glasses with water, then dip the rims of the glasses in the graham cracker crumbs.

Combine the half-and-half, pudding mix, vanilla, and ice in a cocktail shaker and shake until combined and well chilled. Strain into the rimmed glasses, top with the strawberries, and drizzle the syrup over the top. Serve garnished with the mint sprigs.

apple pie à la mode

America's favorite dessert has never been so drinkably delicious! Perfect for sipping after dinner, this smooth and creamy concoction will delight children and adults alike. Those who enjoy alcohol can add a splash of Applejack if they like, but it isn't necessary for appreciating this terrific combination of apple, cinnamon, and vanilla. You can substitute homemade or store-bought chunky applesauce for the pie filling, in which case you'll need to add some sugar to taste. A good-quality vanilla bean ice cream is a must for peak à la mode flavor.

SERVES 2

1 cup canned apple pie filling

²/₃ cup milk

¹/₄ teaspoon ground allspice

4 (¹/₂ cup) scoops vanilla bean ice cream

Lightly sweetened whipped cream, for garnish (page 7)

Ground cinnamon, for garnish

Combine the apple pie filling, milk, and allspice in an electric blender and puree until smooth. Add the ice cream and continue to blend until creamy. Pour into 2 large wine or martini glasses and serve garnished with a dollop of whipped cream and a light dusting of cinnamon.

bittersweet chocolatini

Chocolate cocktails may be all the rage, but let's face it: it's not the alcohol, but the chocolate that makes these drinks so decadently desirable. Deep, dark, and rich are the only ways to describe this chocolate lover's dream made from high-quality melted bittersweet chocolate with just a hint of coffee and vanilla to enhance its flavor. Grated chocolate and cocoa powder rim the glass, and a miniature dollop of whipped cream tops it all off in extravagant style.

SERVES 1

Grated chocolate,
for rimming

Cocoa powder, for
rimming and dusting

2 ounces high-quality
bittersweet chocolate

¹/₄ cup heavy cream

1 tablespoon freshly
brewed coffee

¹/₂ teaspoon alcohol-free
vanilla extract

Ice

Sweetened whipped
cream, for garnish (page 7)

Stir together the chocolate and a little cocoa powder on a plate. Lightly moisten the rim of a martini glass with water, then dip the rim of the glass in the chocolate mixture.

Break the bittersweet chocolate into pieces and put them in a small bowl. Heat the cream in a small saucepan over medium heat until scalding—just until bubbles appear around the edges. Pour it over the chocolate and stir until the chocolate is melted and the mixture is smooth and creamy. Transfer to a cocktail shaker, add the coffee, vanilla, and ice, and shake until combined and well chilled. Strain into the rimmed martini glass and serve garnished with a small dollop of whipped cream and a dusting of cocoa powder.

mint chocolate chip martini

Like an ice cream soda without the fizz and a grasshopper dessert drink without the buzz, this fabulous sweet martini will satisfy any urge for chocolate mint that may arise. Be sure to use a green-colored mint syrup to replicate crème de menthe and a good-quality hot fudge sauce for drizzling. This is a great choice to serve when you have both drinkers and nondrinkers present, as you can easily substitute real crème de menthe for the syrup. Serve in the largest martini glasses you have, with a spoon for scooping.

SERVES 1

1 large scoop mint chocolate chip ice cream

¹/₄ cup light cream

1 tablespoon green mint syrup

1 tablespoon hot fudge sauce, warmed, for drizzling

Mint sprig, for garnish

Put the ice cream in a large martini glass. In a small measuring cup, stir together the cream and syrup, then pour the mixture around, not on top of, the scoop of ice cream. Drizzle the fudge sauce over the ice cream and serve garnished with the mint sprig.

chocolate cream soda

Sometimes the only thing to have with chocolate is more chocolate! And when the weather is hot, a cold drink to accompany dessert may be just the ticket. Serve this with a rich but not overly sweet chocolate dessert, such as chocolate cheesecake or a flourless torte. The chocolate sundae syrup in the soda will happily complement your dessert, while the fizz of the seltzer will help to cleanse the palate between bites.

SERVES 1

3 tablespoons chocolate sundae syrup

3 tablespoons heavy cream

1 cup crushed ice

¹/₄ cup plain seltzer

In a tall glass, stir together the syrup and cream. Add the ice and top off with the seltzer. Serve with an iced tea spoon for stirring and a straw for sipping.

choco coco latte

Dark chocolate, coconut, and cream come together in this decadent dessert cocktail that will wow abstinent guests and compete with any chocolate liqueur others may be savoring. The key ingredient here is the chocolate syrup, which should be a flavoring syrup, not the type used as a dessert topping. Choose one that is rich, dark, and semisweet, such as Torani Chocolate Milano Syrup. Connoisseurs of chocolate will enjoy an accompaniment of international chocolates, such as those whose cocoa beans hail from exotic locales.

SERVES 2

1 cup light cream

2 tablespoons dark chocolate syrup

1 tablespoon cream of coconut

Ice

Semisweet chocolate shavings, for garnish

Combine the cream, syrup, and cream of coconut in a cocktail shaker. Add ice and shake until combined and well chilled. Strain into 2 cocktail glasses and serve garnished with chocolate shavings.

kona koko latte

Kona coffee, grown on the Big Island in Hawaii, is considered by many to be one of the most flavorful coffees around due to its ideal growing conditions. Distinctively fresh tasting, it's the perfect foil for fragrant coconut, as in this luscious latte. Coconut syrup fills in nicely for crème de coconut liqueur, while frothy steamed milk provides additional richness. With its toasted coconut topping, it could serve as dessert itself, although some chocolate-covered macadamia nuts would be a nice complement to its flavor.

SERVES 1

1 cup freshly brewed Kona coffee

¹/₂ cup 2 percent milk

1 tablespoon coconut syrup

Sweetened shredded coconut, toasted, for garnish (see note)

When the coffee is nearly brewed, begin to steam and froth the milk using an espresso machine, or heat the milk in a saucepan and use a manual frother.

Pour the coffee into a large coffee cup and stir in the syrup. Top with the frothy milk. Serve garnished with a sprinkling of toasted coconut.

note: To toast sweetened shredded coconut, preheat the oven to 350°F, place the coconut on a cookie sheet, and bake for 10 to 15 minutes, until lightly browned, stirring occasionally. Cool and store in an airtight container at room temperature, where it will keep for about 2 weeks.

caffè corretto with cream

In Italian coffee bars, Caffè Corretto means your espresso has been "corrected" with a shot of liquor, usually in the form of brandy or grappa. Here, a splash of coffee-flavored syrup—just one of many flavors from which to choose—provides the correction, while a dollop of whipped cream adds a bit of decadence. This as a terrific alcohol-free alternative to coffee and Kahlúa, a popular combination often served with dessert. It pairs perfectly with cake, particularly chocolate cake, or a dish of vanilla ice cream.

SERVES 1

3 ounces freshly brewed espresso

1 teaspoon coffee syrup

Lightly sweetened, softly whipped cream, for garnish (page 7)

Pour the espresso into a small coffee cup or espresso cup. Stir in the syrup and serve garnished with a dollop of whipped cream.

variation: Substitute other flavored syrups such as Irish cream, amaretto, or hazelnut to replicate liqueurs commonly added to coffee.

peppermint white hot chocolate

Here's a creamy and soothing festive finish for any winter get-together. It's a good choice to serve when others are enjoying a hot chocolate laced with peppermint schnapps. White chocolate isn't chocolate in the true sense, as it contains only cocoa butter and no chocolate liquor (a misnomer that refers not to alcohol, but rather to the essence of the cocoa bean). Look for a good-quality white chocolate and avoid any faux versions in the form of vanilla chips or white confection; read the ingredients list to be sure it contains cocoa butter. You can substitute lower-fat milk here, but the result will be decidedly less creamy. Be sure to use a clear peppermint syrup to keep your white hot chocolate white.

SERVES 1

2 ounces white chocolate, chopped

$^1/_2$ cup whole or 2 percent milk

$^1/_2$ cup half-and-half

1 tablespoon clear peppermint syrup

Whipped cream, for garnish

Put the white chocolate in a small bowl. Combine the milk and half-and-half in a small saucepan over medium heat and heat until scalding—just until bubbles appear around the edges. Pour the milk mixture over the chocolate and whisk together until the chocolate has melted and the liquid is slightly foamy. Whisk in the syrup, transfer to a mug, and serve garnished with a dollop of whipped cream.

chapter 5

nightcaps

The term *nightcap* for a bedtime beverage, usually containing a good amount of alcohol, dates back to the eighteenth century, when cold nights required wearing a cap on your head to create warmth—something a few sips of alcohol could also accomplish. Today, a nightcap, frequently brandy or a cream liqueur, may simply cap off the meal or evening or signify that the party or get-together is officially over. But even though alcohol can bring on drowsiness, it doesn't promote restorative sleep, so a cup of chamomile tea or a mug of warm milk is a better bet for saying goodnight and lulling us into a peaceful sleep. Still, when nightcaps are being offered to those who drink alcohol, it's worthwhile to have some special and unique options for abstainers.

From hot toddies to flavorful digestifs—after-meal beverages that assist in digestion—there are many delicious ways to create zero-proof alternatives for everyone to savor. Before long you'll be well versed in concocting the perfect nightcap for family and friends.

spiced apple brandywine

While others sip brandy or cognac, serve this delicious alternative to teetotalers who may wish for something special before they depart. It's both sweet and spicy, with the snappy taste of apple and a hint of grape, and it looks great in a brandy snifter. It's equally tempting when served slightly warm, making it a cozy and soothing conclusion to an evening of autumn or winter entertaining. Look for spiced apple cider in the refrigerated section of your supermarket and be sure to use a not-too-sweet grape juice.

SERVES 2

1 cup spiced apple cider

¹/₄ cup no-sugar-added red grape juice

2 teaspoons aged balsamic vinegar

Pinch of ground ginger

Whisk all of the ingredients together in a small pitcher until combined. If you'd like to serve it warm, whisk all of the ingredients together in a small saucepan and heat until just warm to the touch. Pour into 2 brandy snifters and serve.

caruso comeback

If you or your guests are in need of a tummy comeback after a particularly rich meal, this drink will do the trick. Long known to help calm stomach upset, mint is the highlight in this nod to the classic Caruso after-dinner digestif. You can use either peppermint or spearmint herbal tea here, but be sure to choose green-colored mint syrup for a colorful presentation. When you serve this in vodka glasses or small wineglasses, poured from a decorative decanter, everyone will sing your praises!

SERVES 4

1 cup boiling water

2 herbal mint tea bags

$^1/_2$ cup mint syrup

Splash of tonic water

Pour the boiling water over the tea bags and steep for about 6 minutes, until quite strong. Remove the tea bags, cool the tea to room temperature, then chill before using.

Stir in the syrup and tonic water, transfer to a decanter, and serve in small cocktail glasses.

anisette limon

Anise-flavored liqueurs such as Ouzo and Sambuca have a long history as after-dinner drinks, enjoyed either on their own, in coffee, or with other liqueurs for an ideal digestif. Anise, which has a flavor similar to licorice, and other members in its family of plants, such as fennel, are terrific for settling the stomach, making them perfect for ending an evening of overindulgence. This easy recipe combines anise-flavored syrup with store-bought lemonade for a quaff that will tastefully top off any festivity or celebration in zero-proof style. Opt for a good-quality refrigerated lemonade, such as Newman's Own, rather than frozen concentrate or reconstituted.

SERVES 1

Ice

1 tablespoon anise syrup

1 cup lemonade

Splash of tonic water

Mint sprig, for garnish

Lemon slice, for garnish

Fill a tall glass with ice. Pour in the syrup and lemonade and stir to combine. Top with a splash of tonic water and serve garnished with the mint sprig and lemon slice.

almond roca buona notte

With its flavor of delicious Almond Roca, a buttery almond candy with a hint of chocolate, this nightcap will surely lull anyone into a buona notte (good night) of sleep. Rich and creamy whole milk is called for here, but you can substitute a lower-fat version if you like. Reminiscent of a cup of warm milk with a splash of amaretto and a dusting of cocoa powder, this alcohol-free bedtime delight will warm you from head to toe. One or two Almond Roca candies for nibbling between sips would add to the decadence.

SERVES 1

³/₄ cup whole milk

1 tablespoon Torani Almond Roca Syrup

1 teaspoon light brown sugar

Cocoa powder, for garnish

Heat the milk in a small saucepan over medium heat until scalding—just until bubbles appear around the edges. Remove from the heat and whisk in the syrup and brown sugar. Pour into a heatproof glass or mug and serve garnished with a light dusting of cocoa powder.

scottish tam

In this nod to the hot toddy, a whiskey-based concoction of Scottish origin, the aromatic spices of the unique and ever-popular Constant Comment tea are complemented by sweet honey and tart, healing lemon. Look for a distinctive honey, such as Scottish heather or wildflower, for the best flavor. This soothing remedy is the perfect nightcap to ward off the effects of a blustery winter night.

SERVES 1

1 Bigelow Constant Comment tea bag (regular or decaf)

³/₄ cup boiling water

2 tablespoons heather or wildflower honey

1 tablespoon freshly squeezed lemon juice

Dash of blood orange bitters

Thin slice of lemon, for garnish

Thin slice of orange, for garnish

Put the tea bag in a mug, pour in the boiling water, and steep for 3 to 5 minutes. Remove the tea bag and stir in the honey, lemon juice, and bitters. Serve garnished with the lemon and orange slices.

hot buttered golden slumber

What better way to be coaxed into sleep than with a sweet and buttery natural concoction that will warm and relax you from head to toe. Chamomile, a wonderfully soothing herb for both body and mind, provides the base for this delicious nightcap accented with a hint of lavender aroma to help keep frayed nerves at bay. Keep a batch of the Sweet Spiced Butter on hand for spontaneous nightcap making, and as a delicious spread for toast as well!

SERVES 1

1 chamomile tea bag

1 small sprig of dried culinary lavender

³/₄ cup boiling water

1 tablespoon Sweet Spiced Butter (see recipe below)

Cinnamon stick, for garnish

Put the tea bag and lavender in a mug, pour in the boiling water, and steep until golden, about 3 minutes. Remove the tea bag and lavender, add the butter, stir gently, and serve garnished with the cinnamon stick.

sweet spiced butter

¹/₂ stick (¹/₄ cup) unsalted butter, softened

²/₃ cup firmly packed light brown sugar

¹/₄ teaspoon ground cinnamon

Pinch of ground allspice

Combine all of the ingredients in a small bowl and stir until well combined. Transfer to a piece of plastic wrap and roll up into a small log. Makes abou t ³/₄ cup. Store the butter in the refrigerator, where it will keep for up to 2 weeks.

sweet ginger tummy tea

When drinkers need something to soothe their stomachs, the Italian digestif Cynar may be recommended—an odd-tasting alcoholic elixir made from artichokes, along with other herbs and plants. In this recipe for a magical tummy remedy, the healing power of ginger proves a tastier alternative. Technically not a tea at all, but an infusion of gingerroot, fennel seeds, and cinnamon stick, it will quickly cure nausea and indigestion. Munch on crystallized ginger or ginger snaps between sips, and before you know it, you'll be right as rain.

SERVES 1

1 cup spring water

1 (1-inch) piece gingerroot, peeled and cut into 4 slices

1 teaspoon fennel seeds

1 cinnamon stick

1 heaping tablespoon light brown sugar

Combine all of the ingredients in a small saucepan and bring to a boil, stirring occasionally. Allow to simmer for 1 minute, then remove from the heat. Let the tea infuse for 5 minutes, then pour through a fine-mesh sieve into a mug and serve.

catnap tisane

For the "purr"fect nightcap, look no further than this soothing aromatic drink. Tisanes, which are simply infused hot beverages made by steeping medicinal herbs in boiling water, have been around for centuries and have made use of the healing properties of everything from echinacea to sassafras. In this recipe, chamomile, long treasured for its soothing qualities, is combined with peppermint and catmint to help lull you to sleep. Although famously intoxicating to cats, catnip only has a mild effect similar to chamomile in humans. Prepare the following mix to have on hand so you can quickly steep a cup whenever needed.

SERVES 1

2 teaspoons Catnap Mix (see recipe below)

³/₄ cup boiling water

Honey

Twist of lemon, for garnish

Put the Catnap Mix in a tea ball or use it loose, and place it in a mug. Pour in the boiling water and steep the tea for 5 minutes. Remove the tea ball or strain the tea, stir in honey to taste, and serve garnished with the lemon twist.

catnap mix

1 cup dried chamomile

¹/₂ cup dried peppermint

¹/₂ cup dried catnip (see note)

Combine the herbs in an airtight container and shake gently. Makes 2 cups. Stored in a dark place at room temperature, it will keep for up to 6 months.

note: Before you start digging into Fluffy's catnip stash, visit your local natural food store, where you'll find high-quality organic herbs perfect for making tisanes.

RESOURCES

Many of the ingredients listed below are available at specialty stores such as Williams-Sonoma, Crate and Barrel, Pier 1, Sur la Table, Trader Joe's, Le Gourmet Chef, and Whole Foods. They're also available from the following online retailers.

Almond Roca Syrup and
Chocolate Milano Syrup
www.torani.com

Blood Orange Bitters
www.stirrings.com

Blue Curaçao Syrup
www.monin.com

Blue Raspberry Cocktail Mix and
Sour Apple Cocktail Mix
www.rosesinfusions.com

Elderflower Syrup
www.lepicerie.com

Falooda sev and takmaria
(basil seeds)
www.myspiceshop.com

Lavender
www.lavenderfarms.net

Limonata and Sanbittèr
www.bevmo.com

Orange blossom water, rose syrup, and
rose water
www.cortasfood.com

Pear-infused balsamic vinegar
www.vigoalessi.com

Ricard's Pacific Pastis and Teisseire
Orgeat Syrup
www.frenchfeast.com

Wild Hibiscus Flowers in Syrup
www.wildhibiscus.com

INDEX